*Dedicated to my mother, who gave this book
the most thorough proof-reading imaginable
(and also gave birth to me a while back).*

Introduction

If you were to tell my friends and family ten years ago that I would write a book on habits, they would have laughed. Though I never had any truly destructive habits like using drugs, my everyday habits surrounding productivity and self improvement were abysmal. Even if I had wanted to write such a book, my work habits were so poor that it could have never been completed.

In my late twenties, the illusion of invincibility and goals being reached simply because I wanted them began to wash away. If I was going to reach my goals, something would have to change.

I went to sleep at random hours late at night and woke up in the mid-afternoon. My vehicle registrations and inspections were always delinquent, sometimes by years. I was consistently late to almost everything. The lengths of time by which I procrastinated on important things could be measured in weeks or months. I had half a dozen projects started, none with any real prospect of being finished.

It was obvious to anyone, even myself, that what needed to change was my habits.

Fortunately, I have one trait that rescued me from this abyss of bad habits: when I jump into something, I jump in headfirst and give it everything I've got. I decided that if I was going to tackle habit change, I wouldn't stop until I had mastered it.

I read a lot of books on habit change to understand the underlying mechanics, but more importantly, I experimented on myself relentlessly. Most habit books seemed to be written only for middle-aged businessmen, not young ambitious people with a willingness to push themselves. As I learned more about habits and became more adept at building them, I wanted to push the bounds of determination, willpower, and habit-building.

My only fear was that my life would become too boring if I had this underlying structure of habits. I was willing to accept this trade-off, though, only because I needed good habits so desperately. What surprised me was the freedom which habits gave me. Rather than making me feel like a robot running through routines, building habits has made so much of my life automatic that it feels like I have complete autonomy because I don't have to worry about the basics. They get done in the background.

It doesn't always feel like it, but these days my life is dictated by the habits I've created. When people learn that I write every single day, study a foreign language every day, work on my big projects every day, eat healthy every day, work out every other day, and maintain a consistent sleep schedule, they marvel at the deep well of self discipline that I have. In truth, though, it's all just habits that feel easy. Habits are the closest we can get to having superpowers.

This book is a collection of the mindsets and techniques I've used to rebuild myself with habits. If you, like I used to be, can barely stay on top of the essentials of day-to-day living, this book is for you. If you perform well, but are inconsistent, this book is for you. Or if you're a self-optimizer who already performs at a high level, but wants to squeeze even more out of himself, this book is for you.

BUILDING HABITS

What is a habit, and why are habits so important?

A habit is an outfit a nun wears.

Also, it's an action that you take on a repeated basis with little or no required effort or thought. The power of a habit lies in the second part of that definition– the bit about no required effort or thought. It's a loophole that allows you to upgrade your health, quality of life, productivity, and enjoyment of the world with a fixed expenditure of energy in creating a habit, rather than an ongoing drain on your willpower.

This is the engine that drives the people we most admire: those people who consistently seem to excel at their work, stay healthy, stay connected to those around them, and do all of this while remaining calm and happy. The easy explanation for their success is to say that they're somehow built differently or better than the rest of us, but if they are, it's only because of one key thing: they are better at building and sustaining new habits.

The difference could be represented using a bank account as a metaphor. Those who build habits are like people who live below their means, slowly building up an impressive balance in their bank account. When expenses come up or their situation changes, they're able to cope with it effortlessly by accessing the past deposits (and interest) in their account.

On the other hand, there are people who live paycheck to

paycheck. They never seem to be able to get ahead and every expense is a stretch.

In the short term, the person who lives paycheck to paycheck may not envy the other guy so much. After all, he gets to spend his whole paycheck every week, while the saver seems to be enduring hardship for some unknown purpose.

As time goes on, of course, the saver's position becomes better and better, while the spender's gets worse.

Although it is possible to build your willpower capacity, we all have a limited amount. One who builds habits channels all of his excess willpower to building habits, which pays off later because he's able to sustain those habits without using any additional willpower. On the other hand, some people never build habits, ensuring that they must always rely on available willpower to do anything. This works fine sometimes, but as soon as they're tired or hungry or overworked, everything crumbles.

Don't Spend Your Willpower, Invest It

The glorious benefit of a habit is that it converts something that requires a lot of willpower and focus into something that becomes automatic and often outside of our conscious thought. We can consciously push ourselves to do a only a certain number of things every day, which means that if we don't have good habits, there is a ceiling to what we can accomplish, personally and a professionally. This limit is not particularly high, and is probably not high enough to achieve our goals and live the life we want.

By creating habits, we can move things from the "hard" category to the "easy" category, thus freeing up willpower to tackle more of the hard things. We don't give ourselves the ability to accomplish more by sacrificing health and sanity, which causes burnout, but rather by making some of those hard things easy.

If the idea of being hyper-productive, being physically active and eating right, building good relationships with those around us, learning things that interest you, all while keeping yourself positive and fulfilled seems difficult, it's only because you haven't switched enough of those deliberate actions and attitudes to automatic habits. This takes effort, but establishing most habits takes the relatively short time of one to twelve months.

You Already Have A Million Habits

Saying that we're building habits is a bit of a misnomer. In reality, we are all creatures of habit by design. The vast majority of our daily actions are actually dictated by our subconscious through habits.

Did you brush your teeth this morning? If so, it was because you've built that habit, not because you took fifteen minutes this morning to carefully weigh the pros and cons of dental hygiene. If you procrastinated today, it's because you've built the habit of procrastinating.

Even your outlook on life is the product of your habits. You either have the habit of seeing the positive side of things or the negative side of things, and this single pattern will dominate your mood for the rest of your life. The number of friends you have, and even how much strangers like you upon meeting you, are all the products of habits. Most of our actions stem from subconscious impulse, and those subconscious impulses are the product of our habits.

Because habits are such a fundamental component of who we are, when there is something with which we are discontent, we should examine our habits first. For example, if you aren't happy all of the time, it could be that your life is just terrible, but it's (exponentially) more likely that your set of habits contributes to making you unhappy. Replacing just a few key negative habits with a few positive habits can easily be the difference between being mostly unhappy and being happy almost all of the time.

When we talk about building habits, what we're really doing is replacing the existing habits you have with more useful habits that are aligned with how you want to think and act. You are already an incredible biological machine capable of executing an unlimited number of habits– you just need to have the ones right for you.

Good habits aren't more difficult to execute than bad habits, they're just harder to build

I've lived most of my life as a chronic procrastinator. This was a very easy habit to build, because there were always fun and interesting things available for me to do that didn't involve work. As a child, I'd play computer games instead of doing homework, play outside with my brothers instead of doing chores, and hang out with my friends rather than study for tests. These decisions were very easy to make, so over the years this resulted in my having a very poor work ethic.

When I turned thirty, I had the realization that my then-current work habits would never be sufficient for me to achieve my work goals. Not even close. If those goals were important to me, I'd have to change.

Using the techniques outlined in this book, I did change. I'd love to tell you that it was an easy and overnight change, but it wasn't. I battled with myself and spent the better part of six months destroying my old habit of sloth and replacing it with the habit of industry. This process was hard and it burned up almost all of my daily willpower, especially at first.

Now that I've built a habit of being highly productive, though, it's extremely easy to maintain. I don't even think of it as a difficult thing to work seven days a week, often for twelve hours or more. It's at least as enjoyable as the activities I used to engage in to procrastinate.

In fact, at this very moment I'm on a cruise ship which is specifically designed to contain every possible diversion and method of entertainment, and I'm sitting comfortably, typing away, with no desire to be doing anything else.

The cost of this habit was six months of straining

willpower and mental discomfort. It's a challenging habit to build, and is "priced" accordingly. But is it worth it? Well, for six months of focused effort I now get fifty years or so of loving to work and the enjoyment of the dividends it pays. For me it was unequivocally worth it, but of course as you build your own habits, you'll need to weigh the costs and benefits, which I'll try to lay out as honestly as possible.

New Habits vs. Old Habits

New habits are things that you do, but old habits are things that you are. There's a difference between waking up early and being an early riser, eating a healthy meal and being a healthy eater, getting some work done and being a productive person.

If you want to improve yourself permanently, you must develop more old habits, which is done by creating new habits and sticking with them until they mature into old habits. You know that a habit has crossed that threshold when it becomes something that you subconsciously do, rather than something you must consciously think about doing.

Each new habit strains our willpower, which means that there is a limited number of new habits that we can have at any given time. Old habits, being automatic and subconscious, can be unlimited. So, the ultimate process for self-improvement is to add as many new positive habits as possible, working diligently to convert them to old habits and make room for more new habits.

Think Very Long Term

A habit's power is measured cumulatively. Smoking a single cigarette really isn't very bad for your health, but smoking thousands of them per year adds up and turns smoking into one of the nastier habits you could have. An action whose magnitude is negligible in a single instance becomes a big deal when it's repeated over and over again.

This principle works exactly the same for positive habits. Drinking green tea once won't have any affect on your health, but drinking a few cups every day for years will actually make you a healthier person.

Habits can only be thought of rationally when looked at from a perspective of years or decades. The benefit of a habit isn't the magnitude of each individual action you take, but the cumulative impact it will have on your life in the long term. It's through that lens that you must evaluate which habits to pick up, which to drop, and which are worth fighting for when the going gets tough.

The absolute most important thing in any area is to make sure that your habits are a net positive. If your habits are making you a little bit less healthy every year, you will suffer from health problems and probably die earlier than you have to. If you get a little bit healthier every year, you will probably live a longer life and feel better doing it. It's great to go from becoming a little bit healthier every year to a lot healthier every year, but that change isn't nearly as important as going from becoming a little bit less healthy to a little bit more healthy.

Short-term thinking encourages thoughts like, "Let me push myself to the limit today and get as much done as possible". This results in missing sleep, eating poorly, and a recovery period during which no significant amount of work can be completed. That may lead to better results in the very short term, like the present day, but is making you less productive over longer time horizons.

Consistency Is Everything

When looking through a long-term lens, we can easily see that consistency is the most important factor. Just as it would be better to make 5% interest per year on your financial investments for the rest of your life than 50% interest for one year, it's better to maintain a modest life-long habit than to start an extreme habit that can't be sustained for a single year.

Your results will be commensurate with the consistency with which you execute your habits, not with the magnitude of their one-time impact.

The practical implications of this are twofold. First, be conservative when sizing your new habits. Instead of saying that you will eat a perfect diet for the rest of your life, resolve to cut sugar down by fifty percent. Rather than say you will run every single day, agree to jog home from the train station every day instead of walk, and do one long run every week.

Second, you should be very scared to fail to execute a habit, even once. By failing to execute, potentially you're not just losing a minor bit of progress, but rather threatening the cumulative benefits you've accrued by establishing a habit. This is a huge deal and should not be treated lightly. So make your habits relatively easy, but never miss doing them.

Whenever you are going to skip executing a habit, force yourself to consciously admit that you're skipping, and articulate why you're skipping. It's easy to half-forget to do something, but it's a lot more difficult psychologically to present yourself with a flimsy argument and to go along with it. So if you say to yourself, "Okay, I'm not going to meditate tonight because I'm just too tired," a part of you may challenge, "Even though I am tired, maybe I can just get through it." Try to establish as few "outs" for yourself as possible. We are all creative enough to come up with "good reasons" for not doing something that we don't feel like doing.

Absolutely Never Skip Twice

In the same breath that I caution you to never fail to execute, a realistic view predicts that it will happen from time to time. Any strategy that hopes to create real lasting change must be grounded in reality rather than a Utopian fantasy of what reality could be. You will miss days, you will forget to do things, and in moments of weakness, you will give in to temptation. This happens to even the most grizzled habit builders.

I was talking to a friend about a daily habit that I had. He asked me what I did when I missed a day. I told him about some of my strategies and how I tried to avoid missing a day. What do you do when you miss two days, he asked.

I don't miss two days, I replied.

Missing two days of a habit is habit suicide. If missing one day reduces your chances of long-term success by a small amount like five percent, missing two days reduces it by forty percent or so. Three days missed and you may as well be starting over. At that point you have lost your momentum and have made it far too easy to skip in the future.

This feels like it's not true. It may be easier to be optimistic, to believe that one or two skips in the grand scheme of things aren't a big deal and that you'll surely pick back up tomorrow. But if you skipped once, believed all that, and didn't get back on track the next day, you can no longer trust your assessment.

When you first miss a habit, the next occurrence of it should become a top priority. You must execute on that habit at any level possible. Do it perfectly if you can, but do it terribly if that's all you can handle. Just make sure that you do it.

You can't rely on willpower alone to get through the next day. It didn't work on the first day you skipped, and it's best to acknowledge that it probably won't work the next day. The solution is to plan your day around the habit for the next day. Rather than say, "Okay, I'm definitely going to do it tomorrow", decide specifically when you're going to do it, and come up with solutions to problems in advance, particularly whatever problem stopped you from executing in the first place.

For example, if you've decide that you're going to meditate every single night, but you didn't do it tonight because you were too tired, you might decide that you're going to meditate directly after eating dinner, before you have the chance to get tired.

Plan Variances

When I'm at home, I eat a clean diet of wild caught fish, organic vegetables, grass-fed beef, and whole grains. I eat no sugar, white flour, unhealthy oils, or anything else my research has led me to believe is suboptimal. This is quite easy to do at home when I have full control over my meals, but more challenging while traveling.

For example, while traveling in China for a few weeks, I ate well when healthy food was readily available, but when it wasn't I also ate steamed buns of unknown provenance, random dishes with white rice, and some Chinese sweets. I've also traveled for months eating a clean diet and the cost of doing so includes fairly high levels of inconvenience and being distractingly hungry sometimes.

I don't like to break habits, but when I do break them, I make sure that it's a premeditated and conscious decision. This is the difference between giving up on a habit and losing its benefits, and simply putting it on pause because there are other factors that have a higher value at that time.

When planning a variance, make it concrete, black and white, and specify exactly when the variance will end. For example, instead of doing your regular gym routine while traveling through Europe, you commit to do twenty pushups every morning, and then as soon as you return home, resume your normal routine.

You may be tempted to skip this sort of planning and believe that it is unnecessary, but the lazy energy-conserving part of your brain can be a very powerful enemy. Taking an otherwise acceptable break from a habit can quickly turn into a game of, "Well, I've already missed two weeks of working out— another couple days won't matter", which then evolves into the complete dissolution of a habit you've worked hard to create.

You Just Go – Do a Terrible Job

When we create habits, we're at our best. We're highly motivated, feeling good, and in a low stress period of life conducive to planning. Just because this is the state in which we plan out our habits doesn't mean that it's how we'll feel when we execute on them, however. Just like a marriage, any habit that's intended to last forever will require loyalty through good and bad, sickness and health.

So what do you do when you've promised yourself that you'll write five hundred words every single day, but you're sick, tired, busy, and can't think of a single thing to write about? Just do a terrible job. Write about how bad you feel or about how you don't want to write. If you can't muster the willpower to do either of those things, just write five hundred random words.

Remember that the power of a habit isn't actually in the individual execution, but in the consistency. It is far far worse to skip doing something than to just do a horrible job of it. This feels wrong and sounds counterintuitive, but it's true. Skipping a day makes you feel guilty and unmotivated to do it the next day. Doing a crappy job makes you feel a little bit guilty, but also proud that you worked through a tough time, and eager to improve the next time. Don't believe me? Try it out for yourself.

Don't Reward the Lazy Brain

For all of its glory and genius, your brain can be a stubborn selfish brat sometimes. Until you've fully trained a habit, your brain will try to sabotage you. It does this because the old way was working just fine, and the new way seems like a lot of mental effort. Our brains are designed for efficiency, which sometimes expresses itself as laziness.

The real danger of not following through with something is that your brain figures out that if it just puts a few small barriers in your way, it can go back to resting. This in itself becomes a habit, which you'll see in people that we might call quitters. They have great intentions, good goals, and plenty of ability, but something seems to cause them to quit every single time they start a new campaign. That something is their brain trying to preserve its low-energy efficiency.

A classic manifestation of this is tiredness while working. It is, of course, possible to be tired while working to the point where a nap would solve the problem, but that's very often not an appropriate remedy. I first noticed this when I'd be exhausted, too exhausted to possibly work, as I'd tell myself. I'd stop working and do something less mentally taxing. Within minutes I would be full of energy and wide awake. Rejuvenated, I'd get back to work, only to find that I was tired again.

The solution to this problem is to push through and work anyway. Just do a terrible job if necessary, but make it clear to your brain that putting up token objections isn't enough to give it a rest. If you do this enough, your brain will actually stop trying to sabotage you, and you'll find that you don't get tired when you work, crave sweets when you try to avoid unhealthy foods, or feel like a victim when you should be critically assessing yourself and planning.

Skipped Habits Aren't Excused Habits

My previous flossing habits could best be described as inconsistent. I'd floss once a week or so, occasionally going a week or so without missing a day, but never reached the consistency level necessary to make it a lifelong habit.

Then one day I went to a dentist, found out I had my first cavity, and asked her what I should do differently. She told me that flossing daily was extremely important, even more important than brushing. I already knew that to some degree, but hearing it from an expert convinced me.

I had to change.

With new motivation, I went a couple weeks without missing a single day. Then I went camping, forgot to bring floss, and didn't muster the motivation to ask around to see if anyone else had brought some. I missed a day.

The next day, when I got home, I flossed my teeth twice in a row. I didn't just go over them twice, I flossed, brushed my teeth, then got another piece of floss and did it all over again.

Why would I do that? Was it actually making my teeth any cleaner? Not at all, but I wanted to reinforce to my subconscious that missing a habit wasn't permission to skip it, and that I would still make it up later.

This strategy doesn't apply to everything, of course. If I don't eat healthy today, eating two healthy meals tomorrow won't do me much good, and if I'm late getting somewhere today I can't be doubly on time somewhere the next day. But in cases of things like flossing, meditating, reading, or spending short amounts of time on something, it's a great way to keep the lazy brain in check.

Forgive and Focus

Remember Mister Miyagi from The Karate Kid? He was a tough sensei, working Daniel-san to the bone, and exerting strict discipline on him. He wasn't cruel or petty, though. He loved Daniel-san, truly wanted the best for him, and had faith in him. That's how you want to treat yourself, too.

Missing a habit is bad. Completely giving up on a habit is really bad. The whole point of building habits, though, is to live a better life. If you beat yourself up and lose self-esteem whenever you fail, that negativity will counteract the positivity of building habits.

We all make mistakes. Even if we try to rarely miss, and never skip the second day, and absolutely never quit habits, we will do all of these things at some point. In fact, if you don't make all of those mistakes at various points, you're probably not challenging yourself enough, which means that you will not reach your potential.

Mistakes will happen, but the most important thing is how you react to them. If successes push you forward, but mistakes also push you forward, you will have a lot more forward progress than if success moves you forward but mistakes pull you back.

Use your mistakes to focus. They draw attention to an area that needs more attention, so give it that attention. Challenge yourself to do better next time. Instead of saying, "I'm so bad at this", say "I'm better than this." That's how you use mistakes to your advantage.

Forgive yourself easily, but remember the lessons you learn from mistakes. You've earned them, after all.

Celebrating Success

Everyone knows that rewards work. It's how we train dogs, children, employees, and even ourselves. Yet when most people create habits, they don't reward themselves. They either punish themselves with negative self-talk, or accidentally reward themselves when they fail by giving up. Didn't stick to the diet? Screw it then, let's eat some donuts!

Clearly there are gains to be had by regulating the way we reward and punish ourselves.

Punishment, as described previously, should be productive rather than punitive. But how do we reward ourselves?

My suggestion, which is about as exciting as a parent telling a child that there are apples for dessert, is a simple moment of reflection and a moment of self-congratulation. It sounds lame, but it is the minimum viable reward, it works, and it can be repeated anywhere.

Whenever you stick to a habit, especially if it was difficult or you did particularly well, take two seconds, smile, and congratulate yourself. A fist pump coupled with a "Yes!" might be in order. It feels silly and trite, but it serves its purpose of releasing endorphins and marking progress. It's a reminder to yourself that you're working on something worthwhile and succeeding at it. With the difficulty of building habits and the inevitable slip-ups, these simple rewards can be the difference between enjoying habit change and dreading it to the point of failure.

Small actions like rewarding yourself with a moment of congratulations combine to build a personal system of habit building. Just as any given instance of executing a habit is insignificant compared to the cumulative benefit, every small piece of your habit-building system combines to create a powerful method of improving yourself.

Take Pride in Process, Not in Results

The world is a wonderfully chaotic place, one where incredible amounts of money and time are spent trying to predict outcomes, often with quite poor results. The results of your various endeavors will never be constant and predictable, but rather will always be filled with at least as much signal as noise.

Beyond the inherent randomness in life is the fact that progress lags behind action. If you eat perfectly healthy for a week, you may not lose any weight at all. But if you eat well for years, you can make a safe bet that you will be in better shape, be healthier, and feel better than if you hadn't. Most habits worth having are long-term ones.

The one constant in your life is yourself. You have full control over your actions, even if those actions don't guarantee any given result once they're subjected to the outside forces of the world.

When evaluating your progress in building habits, you need something consistent to grade yourself against. Use your adherence to process, not your actual results. So if you're trying to lose weight, evaluate yourself based on how well you stick to your plan rather than the number on the scale, especially in the short term.

Focusing on results, especially short term results, is an excellent way to add stress to your life. That could lead to you quitting the habit associated with that stress, thus ensuring no long term results are ever achieved. Track your adherence to process, not your results.

CHOOSING HABITS

Being Honest

The core skill required for choosing habits, as well as for staying on track once a habit is implemented, is the ability to be brutally honest with oneself. Being brutally honest is very different from being brutal. It means that you are only satisfied when you figure out which bad habit is really holding you back from your goals, and then you attack that habit by replacing it with a better one.

Being honest with oneself requires a lot of self-trust. Some people are unable to identify their own weaknesses because they will criticize themselves and weaken their own self-esteem. This leads to an inability to self-diagnose and overcompensation in other areas, usually by putting other people down. While possibly effective at increasing self-esteem in the short term, this strategy all but prohibits substantial long-term growth.

It is difficult for most of us to admit that we are failing to meet our own standards, especially in areas tied to our self-esteem. It may be extraordinarily difficult to admit to yourself that you're out of shape, not on a trajectory that will lead to enough wealth to support a family, or unable to socialize effectively. That admission creates vulnerability within yourself, which is made public when others notice that we're trying to change.

Admitting to yourself that you've failed to meet your own standard can also create internal tension. After all, the only two choices are undergoing massive change to meet those standards, or realizing that you're unwilling to rise to the occasion.

This may all sound difficult and unpleasant, and it is those things, but it is also the first step towards building the most effective habits. It's easy to create habits to improve marginally at things you're already good at, but it's much more difficult to cut to the heart of the issue and begin a new habit that addresses a fundamental core weakness.

I've gone through this process personally in three major areas. At one point I realized that I was so introverted and shy that it was unlikely I would ever have a dating life that would be fulfilling. Admitting that was difficult and embarrassing, and the path it lead to was filled with rejection and unraveling layer after layer of inadequacy. Three years ago I had a similar revelation about my work habits. I had achieved moderate success, but had to face the truth that my work habits were not nearly strong enough to reach all of the goals I had set for myself. The result was three years of putting more effort into my work than I had in the preceding twenty-nine years. Last, about a year ago I admitted that I was physically weak, and I sought the help of an expert to help me build up strength.

This lead to spending hours at the gym and eating more protein-rich foods than I'd ever consistently eaten before.

Being honest with myself was difficult in all of these cases, and in each scenario it led to even more pain in the form of discomfort and effort through new habits. The results have been worth it, though, and could never have been achieved without that initial step of being honest with myself.

How to Discover High Priority Habits

Choosing your next habit is a personal decision, sort of like choosing a house or a spouse. While there may not be an exact scientific process for choosing the best one, there are guidelines to steer you in the right direction.

The easiest time to choose a habit is when something is a major impediment in your life, or where there's one habit that currently extends its negative influence into other areas of your life. If you smoke or eat unhealthy food, those would be obvious first choices.

However, the right habit to tackle is one that you care about. If you aren't convinced that the benefits of quitting smoking exceed the downsides, it's not the right habit for you now. The difficulty of the habit in question is far less important than how much it means to you.

While I suggest a top-down approach to habit building, picking off the big ones and then going for the little ones, motivation often works the other way around. Sometimes building small habits can build momentum and self-confidence that gives people the strength and motivation to tackle the larger ones. So shoot for big habits first, but don't be discouraged if you're not ready for them. The best habit is the one you can succeed at, which paves the way for a lifetime of habit building.

Let's say that you've picked off all of the obvious habits. You've overcome weaknesses you've lived with forever and you've built a new set of habits that's serving you well. Now what?

One idea is to ask your friends. I have really high-performing friends with great habits, but I could probably point out a glaring-to-an-outsider habit for about half of them. Having the courage to ask what you need to work on can yield some really huge wins that you won't otherwise get to.

Another place to look is in those categories that "just aren't you". Maybe you're really scrawny and weak like I was, so weightlifting never crossed your mind. Maybe you're a type-A hustler and you've never thought about yoga or meditation. Or maybe you're a free-spirit who's never thought about building up a stronger work ethic.

One area to examine in particular is social skills. Unlike almost any other arena, and despite having the word "skills" in the name, we think of social skills as magical gifts we're born with– or not. Building social skills, something very few people actually do, pays off immensely. As much as we may like to imagine ourselves as islands at times, so much of the quality of our lives and external impact will be determined by our interactions with others.

The first phase of habits, countering your weaknesses, makes you the best version of yourself. Exploring areas that "just aren't you" is how you expand how you define yourself and take things to the next level. You become more rounded and versatile, but you also find connections between various habits. Spending time with ballet and programming, two nearly polar opposite practices, allowed me to really examine how I learn things, as that was the only common thread between the two.

If you've gotten to the point where you've got the basics covered and you've rounded yourself out, choose whichever habits seem the most fun to you, even if they don't seem very useful. You'll be so adept at this point at building habits, that the enthusiasm for habits that interest you will often be enough to load new habits very quickly.

It's Always Your Fault

Most people go through life with the attitude that negative things that happen to them are not their fault. People are quick to claim the role of victim, but never of unjust aggressor. Like the more general habit of self-deception, this tendency is not conducive to building habits. Instead, it's best to assume that it's always your fault.

Not happy? Assume that it is your fault. Not in shape? Assume that it is your fault. Not as wealthy as you'd like to be? Assume that it is your fault. Don't have as many friends as you'd like, get sick frequently, or live in a messy house? All your fault.

Not everything is actually your fault, but by assuming it is, you give yourself an opportunity to take responsibility for the future by coming up with a plan to change things. You also over-correct for the bias we all have against believing we are responsible for negative outcomes.

To say that something is your fault, or that it is someone else's fault, is an oversimplification. Circumstances are usually more nuanced and tangled than that. Perhaps you were robbed, and you blame that event for your poverty. Being robbed was certainly a factor, but cannot be the only factor. Did you do anything that made it possible to be robbed? Why didn't you recover faster? Assuming that everything is your fault is a shortcut for finding those areas where you have control, and opening the door to exerting that control for positive change.

That's not to say that you should feel guilty about any of these things. Transgressions against others should probably be accompanied by enough guilt to prompt you to make things right, but self-inflicted wounds should be treated with compassion.

Rather than guilt, discoveries of potential fault should be seen as major opportunities. After all, when you find something in your life that you aren't happy with, and you assume responsibility for it, that also implies a power to change it. What is a habit if not a tool to change things about ourselves that leave room for improvement?

There's Nothing You Can't Do

I used to believe that those who were extremely successful, whether it be in business, love, physical accomplishment, or any other arena, were cut from a different cloth. I thought that they were born with some sort of magic. Improve as I may under my own devices, I could never reach their heights.

Over the years I have had the good fortune of coming face to face with many of those people who seemed to be superhuman. I've been friends with some of the most successful musicians of my generation, some of the most socially skilled people, and some of the most successful businesspeople. In every single case, I've been awed by one thing- how normal they are.

My stubborn preconceptions were slowly worn away as I came to understand that people we think of as exceptional aren't that way because of who they are, but because of what they do. In every single case they had a set of habits that led them to the top of their fields. In most cases their natural proclivities created those habits for them, but I've also seen plenty of examples of people systematically rewiring their habits to orient themselves for success.

You can do just about anything if you break it down into habits and execute on them. That's not to say that it's easy, only that it's possible. The key is to be honest about what's stopping you from success, take responsibility for it, and create new habits to correct.

For example, the world is full of aspiring musicians who believe that what's holding them back from success is that one connection who will showcase them to the world. That's not how the musicians I've known made it, though. They repeatedly improved their craft, took responsibility for their own success, identified their own weaknesses and turned them into strengths. That's the process by which greatness is developed.

Addition Versus Subtraction

Fundamentally, there seem to be two types of people: those who find it easier to add new behaviors, and those who find it easier to subtract them. A simple test is to think about whether it's easier for you to cut out junk food or to go to the gym. Those who prefer to go to the gym are adders, and those who cut out junk food are subtracters.

I found it relatively easy to cut out all unhealthy foods, but it required a lot of willpower for me to get to the gym on a regular basis. I'm a natural subtracter.

It is undoubtedly a good thing to work on both the ability to be an adder and subtracter. However, there's no harm in leaning on your strengths when constructing habits, particularly when beginning work on a new area or when attacking a failed habit from a different angle.

As an extreme example, when I wanted to date more, with the first step being going out and talking to more women, I made a list of six things I was allowed to do (work, eat, sleep, read after midnight, play violin, talk to women), intentionally making it so that talking to women was the most fun thing I was allowed to do. Through subtracting I got myself to add.

Be aware of which approach you prefer and avoid being a slave to it, but be willing to rely on it during difficult phases of habit building.

Don't Overshoot

Habit forming is effective and efficient, but it's not effortless. Habits should always be linked to an actual concrete goal, rather than just exist for the sake of having a habit. In other words, don't eat healthily because it sounds like a nice habit, eat that way because you want to live longer, be more capable of physical activity, or improve your appearance.

An important component of having a goal tied to a habit is that it allows you to size your habit proportionally to the goal. If you want to lose weight to look better, maybe you need to lose one pound per month for a year. That will allow you to create an easily sustainable habit that will get you to your goal and still leave you plenty of capacity for other habits or obligations on your time and willpower.

When I picked up violin, I was in the middle of an intense work cycle which demanded every bit of my will and time. Thinking about what I wanted out of playing the violin, I recognized that I would be content to just have one good piece that I could play, primarily to give my brain a quick break from work when I needed it.

So rather than buy an expensive violin, sign up for

weekly lessons, and start from the beginning, I got a hand-me-down violin, found a tutor, and had him teach me, over the course of a few lessons, learned one piece I liked to mediocrity. Rather than dedicate hours to practice every day, I used spare minutes where I needed to step away from the computer to run through the piece once or twice.

In the end, I received the fulfillment of learning to play the violin, but didn't spend more time or effort on that pursuit than was necessary to reach my goals. That's not to say that a habit of practicing violin for eight hours a day isn't a great habit– it just wasn't the right habit for my goal.

Securing Your Motivation

Excitement and motivation are different entities, but can easily be confused in the early stages of a habit. Excitement is like the energy that powers a sprinter, powerful and available immediately, but in danger of running out after a short while. Motivation is like the energy that powers a marathon runner, less powerful over any given increment, but capable of lasting much longer.

Excitement is enough to get you through the first week or two of a new habit, but is fundamentally unable to sustain you beyond that. To go further, you need real motivation. Failing to understand and validate your motivation up front leads you to the possibility of entering a cycle of pushing hard on a new habit for a couple weeks, losing interest, feeling bad for giving up, and then being slightly more reluctant and pessimistic towards future habits. This pattern must be avoided.

If you are not going to follow through with a habit, it is better to never start it at all. A downward spiral of failing to adopt habits is harmful in the long term, and the time spent on a habit that never had a chance could have been better spent on a properly motivated habit that would have been successful. Whenever you feel like you may not have proper motivation for a habit, pick a new one and revisit the discarded habit later on.

The very first tangible step in creating a new habit is understanding exactly why you're drawn to it. The skill of being brutally honest with oneself is critical at this stage. If you want to start a habit of eating healthy foods because your health is important to you and you want to live as long as possible to be there for your family, that motivation will sustain you through the hard times of the habit. On the other hand, if you want to eat healthy foods because your friend called you fat, that probably won't sustain you.

It's important to remember that excitement will be the dominant force in your habit-building in the beginning, but it will eventually wane and you will be forced to rely on your true motivation. Ask yourself whether, under duress and the pressures and chaos of the real world, your motivation will still be strong a month from now and a year from now. If the answer is no, do not start the habit, or at least scale the habit back in intensity.

Maybe the motivation will be sufficient to avoid eating ice cream, but not enough to cut out all fast food. If that's the case, be honest with yourself and size your habit accordingly. In most areas of life, it's better to try and to fail than to not try at all. In establishing habits, it's far better to succeed at an easier habit and then build up from there.

Discovering Motivation

Sometimes you have to create a new habit due to outside pressures, but you don't have a burning desire to implement it. The chance of success under these conditions is slim, so you must learn to discover motivation.

On a piece of paper, write down these four sections:

1. What good things will happen if I implement this habit?
2. What bad things will happen if I implement this habit?
3. What good things will happen if I don't implement this habit?
4. What bad things will happen if I don't implement this habit?

For any given habit, you should be able to think of several things for each category. Those in sections 1 and 4 will be motivating, but 2 and 3 will be demotivating. You might be tempted to only list the motivating ones, but this will backfire because you will no longer trust your list. So write things in every section. When you see that the positives outweigh the negatives, you will have an honest and sober assessment of your options and a clear winner.

Keep in mind that one significant positive thing might counteract several smaller negative ones. It's important to read over the list carefully and visualize each outcome to feel its impact. Which do you want the most? Which are you the most afraid of?

Allowing your mind to really go through each item and imagine what life would be like under each circumstance, implementing the habit or not, creates a visceral drive to adopt the habit.

To make sure that this motivation sticks, write yourself a note explaining why you're going to implement the habit. This sounds incredibly corny, but it's also effective, and that justifies it in my estimation.

Eight years ago I decided that I wanted to switch to a sleep schedule where I slept for fifteen minutes every four hours instead of eight hours at night. The schedule would shave six hours of sleep time off per day and was reported to leave people completely rested, after a brutal transition period.

On day two I wrote myself a semi-delirious rambling letter about all of the great things that would happen when I switched to the schedule, and all of the bad things that would happen if I didn't. In retrospect, the letter is tremendously embarrassing; but at the time it worked.

Whenever I'd be exhausted and want to quit, I'd read the letter, feel some of the enthusiasm, and one or two of the points would hit home and keep me going. Maybe more than anything, I knew that I could trust my analysis at the time, and would follow my own reasoned guidance.

Start Easy and Often

Say you've decided that you're just too stressed out and prone to impulse and that the appropriate habit to develop is to meditate for thirty minutes every other day. That sounds smart and reasonable, but what if you seriously worry that when the excitement wears off and the stresses of life build up, you may not stick to meditating for the full amount of time on schedule?

You'll get the greatest compliance by maximizing frequency and minimizing intensity. Daily habits are hard to overlook or miss, and low intensity habits are easy to complete. This combination greatly increases your chances of sticking with a habit.

Once you have any level of success, it's easy to build upon it to strengthen the habit. So maybe instead of starting with thirty minutes every other day, you resolve to meditate for just one minute every single day. This sounds ridiculous, and probably won't bring you any tangible benefits on its own, but once it becomes part of your life, doubling it to two minutes is also very easy. Then you increase to five minutes, then ten, then fifteen. Once you get there, you'll be so used to meditating that cutting the frequency to every other day while doubling the duration to half an hour will be manageable.

With this schedule of a small start with regular increases, you won't be reaching your full goal for a long time, maybe several months or even a year. If you're thinking short-term, you may discard this idea. If you think long-term, though, you realize that just having the habit is the most important part, and that the cumulative benefits of even a reduced intensity meditation habit will be far greater than those from an aborted, intense habit that lasts only a couple weeks.

Start small, become consistent, and increase at a manageable pace. That's how you optimize for the finish line, rather than the starting line.

The Magic of Daily Habits

Whether for small or big habits, bias yourself strongly towards habits which require daily execution. There are several factors in play that counter-intuitively make daily habits the easiest to maintain.

A serious danger to the habit builder is the reasonable reschedule. Let's say that you've decided you're going to clean your house every Sunday. One Sunday, though, you have a dinner party that extends into the late evening. With more work to do than usual and less energy to do it with, you decide to clean up Monday instead.

As a busy person, however, you already have a full day booked for Monday. So while it was easy to imagine you cleaning up the night before when you were exhausted, the practical task of finding time to clean during an already packed day is much more difficult. The task gets pushed for a few more days, and finally you decide to just skip that week and do it the following Sunday.

Each decision along the way was rational, in the short run, but the combination of that downward spiral of decisions threatens the existence of your new habit to clean on Sunday.

Daily habits, on the other hand, are resistant to the reasonable reschedule. If you say that you're going to clean every single day, you can't just push the habit by a day. Instead, you are skipping a day, something you should be building an extraordinary aversion to. Even though it leads to failure in the long run, the reasonable reschedule feels like a partial success. Skipping does not.

The daily habit also earns a place in the front of your consciousness. It's hard to juggle complex weekly and irregular schedules, but we all know the basic things we must do each day. It takes a couple weeks of compliance, but it's daily habits will quickly become an indelible part of your daily must-do list. I've written every day for the past nine months or so. If I didn't write today, something would feel wrong, just as if I forgot to brush my teeth.

Last, daily habits can often be quite small. The amount of time required to clean a house that was just cleaned twenty-four hours ago is usually minimal. The urge to push or skip a small task is much smaller than a large one. It's more likely that reasons for skipping these smaller tasks will not be physical, but psychological, which we can work on. If you need five hours to clean but only have two, you have to skip. If you need thirty minutes but don't feel like spending that time, you can convince yourself to suck it up and be a champion.

Don't Build Habits That can be Automated

The primary reason we build habits is to ensure that things are done on a regular basis. To do this we move repeating tasks from our conscious mind to our subconscious mind, so that they happen automatically. For some tasks, though, we can take things a step further and completely automate them outside of our own consciousness.

This may seem like a lazy approach, and it could be, but if you use your freed-up willpower and time to build another habit, it's an effective approach.

A minor daily habit of mine used to be to check two websites for good flight deals. This wasn't a good habit in that it was making me a more effective person, but it allowed my friends and me to go on more trips than we'd normally be able to, which was a big positive in my life.

One day I decided to see if I could write a small computer program to automatically search these sites and send me the results whenever a new flight deal showed up. It worked, and for the past year or so I've had an extra few minutes every day, as well as one less thing to think about.

Another example would be automating your credit card payments so that cards automatically get paid in full on their due dates. As long as you're confident you'll always have enough money in your account, that's a decent-sized mental burden you can completely erase.

Prime candidates for automation tend to be these sorts of habits, those that are less about personal change and more about things that just "have to be done" on a regular basis. Saving a minute or two here and there isn't a big deal, but the cumulative benefit of removing things from that mental todo list is big. It's the difference between constant distraction, wondering if there's something critical that needs to be done, and having a clear mind for whatever tasks and habits you have each day.

Loading and Maintenance

If you lift weights, you're probably familiar with the supplement creatine. It allows your muscles to hold more water, which helps them lift more, which in turn breaks down muscle fiber more quickly, which allows you to build muscle more quickly.

For creatine to be effective, you must have a certain amount of it in your bloodstream. To get it there, you take a loading dose for a short period of time, usually a week or ten days. Then, once you've built up a baseline level of creatine, you drop the dose to a fraction of the loading dose and take this maintenance dose every day.

Habits work the same way. Humans are creatures of routine, and altering that routine takes significantly more willpower and effort than simply maintaining it. For that reason, you'll often want to have one very strict habit for loading, and then another to maintain. Put in the effort up front and then make it easy.

When I decided to eat healthy food, I was coming from a very poor diet. I didn't eat much fast food, but I had no problem eating lots of sugar, white flour, poorly raised meat, and unhealthy oils. Because I'd been eating all my life, my habits around eating were very well established. To truly replace those habits with new ones, rather than just cover them up with temporary willpower-fueled activities, I had to be severe.

For three years, I ate no white flour, sugar, poorly raised meat, or bad oils. Even as I traveled around the world, I would spend inordinate amounts of time sourcing good restaurants and grocery stores. If I couldn't find good food, I would go hungry. I remember the one and only time I cheated, where I ate a small bag of white rice on a 25 hour train across Cambodia, because I was famished and it was the healthiest food available.

I knew that this wasn't sustainable in the long term, but I also knew that it was the only way I could really recalibrate my brain to prefer healthy foods. This was my loading habit.

Now I'm more flexible. When I travel, I eat a fair amount of unhealthy food. When I'm at home, I eat a strict diet except for one meal on Sundays with friends. This is my maintenance habit, and it's sustainable forever as far as I'm concerned.

How do you know when to switch from your loading habit to your maintenance habit? The key is to be able to honestly evaluate what would happen if you dropped the habit entirely. If you think that you would immediately go back to your old ways, keep loading. If you think that you would either slowly slide back to your old ways over a period of months or years, or if you think you'd remain in stasis, switch to a maintenance habit.

The purpose of the loading habit is to completely remove all associations with your old habit. You start small, build up to your loading habit, keep at it until you believe that your new behavior is fixed in place, and then switch to maintenance.

Often times you'll reach your goals during the loading phase. Your aim with maintenance is to keep the benefits and to continue to get better, even if that improvement is slight. If you're not getting slightly better, you're getting slightly worse, which will eventually unravel the habit.

Using the diet example, you might start by cutting out sugar on weekdays, then on weekends, then cut out white flour on the same schedule, then low-quality meat, then unhealthy oils. Maybe that takes a full year. You then stay on your complete abstinence diet for a year or two, until you truly prefer that way of eating. At that point you switch to maintenance which still dictates mostly healthy meals, but allows exceptions for special occasions. That diet would help you reach your short-term goals, but would also leave you with a sustainable plan that would continue to improve your health for the rest of your life.

This two-phase habit system also makes adherence easier. Disrupting entrenched habits requires a period of hardcore adherence, but knowing that it won't last forever helps you to mentally get through the most difficult times.

The Habit of Building Habits

Everything is a habit, including the habit of constructively building habits. You'll find that the first few habits you deliberately introduce into your life will take a lot of effort, and may even feel like they weren't worth it. It's important to remember that the very act of building these habits, hard as it may be, will make building future habits easier.

So although the effort to build the first simple habit may not be worth it in isolation, it is worth it when you add in the benefit of the next habit being slightly easier to build, and the next one afterwards even easier than that.

To get the most out of the habit-building process, pay close attention to where you have the most difficulty. Some people may have trouble digging down to their true motivation for wanting to implement a habit, others may have trouble choosing the best habits for them at any given time, and others may have trouble sticking with the habit.

When you notice patterns in where you fall short, exercise brutal honesty and account for your weakness in the future. Maybe you need to spend more time actually writing out your motivations, you need an honest friend to give you some guidance on where your efforts could best be spent, or you need someone to hold you accountable. By finding these weaknesses and working on them, you make your likelihood of future habits becoming successful much higher.

Triggering Habits

If we think about common negative habits, we easily accept that they have specific triggers. Stress triggers overeating or gambling, waking up might trigger smoking, or boredom might trigger wasting time online. Even though we're conscious of these triggers, we don't put much thought into triggering positive habits. Why not use such a powerful reality of the human experience to our benefit?

When you wake up in the morning, that is a trigger for a habit, whether you've thought of it that way or not. You probably do just about the exact same thing every morning, assuming that trigger is the same, although waking up late on a weekend may be a different trigger than waking up to an alarm during the week. Getting home from work or school is another trigger you probably already have. Same with situational triggers like receiving bad news, having to wait in a line, or getting onto a train.

Without a proper trigger, a repeated action is just something you sometimes do. Meditating once in a while when it strikes your fancy is an inconsistent hobby. Meditating every single day when you wake up is a habit.

Whenever you begin a new habit, you should think about what its trigger is going to be, and to commit to that. Don't say that you will drink tea every morning, because you probably won't. Say that every day, as soon as you wake up, you will drink tea. You can even write "First, drink tea" on a post-it note and put it on your alarm clock to ensure consistency as you build the trigger.

The hidden benefit is that you can only have one action most-strongly linked to any given trigger, so this is also a good way to get rid of bad habits. If you have the habit of browsing gossip sites whenever you turn on your computer, and you retrain yourself to respond to open emails as soon as you turn on the computer, you both gain a new good habit and lose a old bad one.

This is also possible with situational triggers, although they are a little more difficult to identify. People who overeat may not realize that they do so when they become stressed. An honest and introspective look at when you most often exhibit your bad habits can help you find triggers primed for reprogramming.

If you realized that you overeat as a way of coping with stress, you'd want to find a more productive way of dealing with that stress to replace the old one. So you might tell yourself, "Okay, whenever I feel stressed, or feel like I'm about to be stressed, I'm going to drink a cup of green tea, write out what's worrying me the most, and then take one small step towards resolving it."

Articulating your exact plan for that trigger helps make it concrete in your brain. There's a big difference between doing that and thinking, "Okay, I shouldn't overeat when I'm stressed." One is replacing a trigger with a healthier one, and the other is just the acknowledgment of a problem without offering yourself a tangible solution.

Just as we all have millions of habits, whether we recognize them or not, we all have millions of triggers as well. Some are strong triggers that always cause the same reaction, while others are weak ones that might just incline you towards certain actions. Either can be reprogrammed to have a strong association with a positive habit.

From this soup of unknown habits and triggers we are able to consciously rewire ourselves to make excellent subconscious choices which move us closer to our goals. Because we're using existing triggers and are designing manageable habits, this huge improvement can be made with relatively little ongoing effort and drain on willpower. We're not adding more triggers to our days, we're just changing the actions they spur.

Chaining Habits

You can also use habits as triggers for other habits, thus creating a reliable chain. For example, when I wake up, the very first thing I do is put a pot of water on the stove. Putting the water on is a trigger to brush my teeth, so I do that while it boils. Once it's done, I make tea and sit down at my desk. That's a trigger for me to read my email, check my calendar, and check various reports and stats that may affect how I plan my day.

When I'm done with all that, I allow myself to browse my favorite sites, but finishing my tea is a trigger to get to work. If I feel tired while I work, that's a trigger to drink some water, a trigger I reprogrammed from my previous default of lying on my bed and possibly taking a nap.

My entire day isn't one giant long chain, but there are some core sequences. Waking up is one, and the clock hitting midnight, signaling the end of my workday, is another.

A very good practice is to think about all of the things that absolutely must get done in a day, and work them into chains. Unless the order actually matters, the easiest habits should be loaded up front, and the most difficult ones should be last. This ensures that you maximize the benefit of momentum as you move through your chain. If my chain started with four hours of work and then ended with tea and brushing my teeth, you can imagine how hard it would be to get started and how easy it would be to skip things like tea.

Moving through your chain, even once it becomes routine and ordinary, is very satisfying. You know that it will accomplish the major requirements of your day, yet it becomes so automatic that it feels effortless. It's through this process that habits give you freedom– chains take care of the necessities of life, and leave you with time and willpower to make forward progress.

The danger of chaining is that when your schedule is disrupted to make the first step or two impossible, your compliance with the rest of the chain will drop off precipitously. I notice this the most when I'm traveling. I don't travel with stuff to make tea, so often the first thing I do is browse the internet. Because I don't have finishing my tea to serve as a trigger for getting to work, I can end up wasting too much time surfing online.

I don't have a perfect solution to this. I've experimented with alternative chains for traveling, which works well on long trips where you can actually establish a temporary set of habits, but doesn't work for short travel or rapid travel through several locations. Just being aware of things like travel, which interfere with your habits and chains, can be useful. You can use that disruption as a trigger to be vigilant and remind yourself that the road ahead will be temporarily more difficult.

When appropriate, sacrifice your maintenance habits in favor of keeping up your loading habits. You might let your diet slip because you've been on it for years, but make a point of writing five-hundred words every day because that's a new habit that hasn't gotten a toehold yet. Maintenance habits will very quickly slip back into place on the chain when you're able to return to it, but I've found loading habits to feel like big impositions and sometimes completely fall off.

Chains are a powerful tool to make organizing series of habits effortless, but it's important to remember that the links of the chain are more important than the chain itself. Don't allow a break in the chain to ruin all if its components. Allow chains to serve as shortcuts to habit-building, but don't let them prevent you from executing on habits when they break.

Accountability With Friends

In many areas of life there's a battle between doing the

thing that will work very effectively to solve a specific problem in the short term versus doing that which will take longer to become effective but will solve many problems in the long term. For example, building up willpower is extremely slow, but once you have a high capacity for it, you can do a lot of difficult things outside your routine. If you have low or normal willpower, you will rely exclusively on habits to get a lot done.

Similarly, it's a good practice to build up the ability to be accountable entirely to yourself, but if you're unable to do that, or for habits that are very long term or very difficult, you can ask a friend to help you be accountable.

A good friend of mine, Leo Babauta, who is a master of habits and is excellent at being accountable to himself, asked me to help him stay accountable for his diet because he was trying to eat a perfect diet for a full six months. That's a very difficult challenge, but having someone to stay accountable to makes it slightly easier.

Earlier this year I wanted to completely eliminate all non-work web browsing for three months, so I asked a friend to hold me accountable. It worked, and I'm not sure I would have been able to do it without him.

When asking a friend to hold you accountable, make it concrete and easy for him. It must be concrete, because you don't want to impose on him to constantly evaluate your progress. Either Leo ate sugar or he didn't. Either I visited a web site or I didn't. You must also report your progress at regular intervals. Leo created a shared spreadsheet where I could see whether he ate properly each day.

Last, there must be consequences for failure. The primary purpose of having consequences is that they make the agreement official and definite. People remember bets, but forget offhand claims. My friend bet me $50 I couldn't stay off the web sites for three months. Without the bet, I doubt he would have kept track of it if he had just said, "I don't think you can do it". Since your friend is doing you a favor, be willing to make a one-sided bet where he has no downside.

Reserve accountability for only the most difficult and important of your habits. It increases compliance, but at the cost of coordinating (albeit minimally) with someone else. It's also a missed opportunity to build the habit of self-reliance, so use it only when there's serious concern that you may not stick with the habit without it.

Habitualizing Input for Instant Change

When we talk about creating habits, we are talking about changing our long-term behavior. We extrapolate our current trajectory, decide we would prefer a different trajectory, and then we take the steps to bend reality towards it.

In an ideal world, the mere conception of a new trajectory would be enough to immediately make it reality. In practice, there's typically the loading period before a habit takes root and we can switch to just maintaining it.

The only exception I've experienced is when a habit is

underpinned by a strong belief and that belief changes.

Up until my mid-twenties, I ate a very unhealthy diet. My parents tried their best to feed me healthy food, but I was a picky eater, and once I had freedom, I chose fast food, sweets, and fried things. My belief was that I was skinny, didn't have cavities, and felt fine, so there was no point in eating healthy food.

When I was twenty-five, I read a book that explained the long-term implications of eating unhealthy food, down to the molecular level. I learned specifically why each unhealthy food was bad, how it affected my body, and what I could expect long-term if I kept eating it. I may stay skinny and never get a cavity, but I would eventually succumb to disease.

Acquiring this new knowledge created a quantum shift in my beliefs regarding my habits. My triggers changed. Unhealthy food no longer prompted a desire for the hedonistic pleasure of consumption, but instead sparked a revulsion towards the path my life might follow if I ate that food.

Overnight my appetite for unhealthy food vanished, and I became a healthy eater. I codified my new diet, adhering to which served as a maintenance habit, and I changed overnight. That's not to say that there weren't moments of temptation and tweaks to the diet to make it healthier or more convenient.

The tricky bit about these belief-triggered instant changes is that you can't actively search for them. I believed that my views on diet were correct, so I would never purposefully look to contradict them. I only read the book about healthy eating at the insistence of a friend who had often steered me in the right direction.

Still, these instant changes are so powerful that we'd be foolish not to try to maximize them. How can we do that?

The first key is to be open-minded, something with which I've personally had difficulty. The habit I use to combat this is to use the trigger of strong disagreement to ask, "Is it possible he's right? What if he is?" I'm stubborn enough that this usually won't change my opinion, but it's enough to cause me to reflect and sometimes realize that I'm wrong.

The next method to maximize these sorts of realizations is to habitualize exposing ourselves to positive influence. We tend to focus habits on what we do, rather than what we take in. If we fail to direct attention to input, we can still improve significantly, but have only limited avenues for growth. Maximum growth comes when we allow ourselves to consider high-quality influence, contemplate it, and use it to direct habits and action.

One particularly valuable habit in this regard is reading every single day. You will consume so many books that you're bound to run into some that contradict your beliefs and occasionally run into one that changes your perception in an instant and births a new lifelong habit.

When to Quit Habits

As mere fallible human beings, even the most considerate among us are going to begin habits that don't serve us as we expect, aren't worth the effort of installation, or have unintended negative consequences. How do we know when to quit them?

It's a serious consideration, because it's important that we err on the side of not quitting habits. Without that bias, it's far too likely that we'll quit a habit just as it gets difficult, but before it pays off. Quitting at that point creates a negative cycle of failure, makes future habits harder to implement, and ensures that we exert maximum effort for the minimum in results. In other words, it's a medium-sized disaster.

The solution is to only quit habits when you no longer want to quit them. This is the only mindset under which we can make difficult decisions and not be influenced by our pesky lazy brain. This point will never be found in the loading period, only some time during the maintenance period.

A week into my habit of lifting weights three times a week, I wanted to quit. My morale was low, I'd seen no results (as expected, of course), and I was cognizant of how much time I was devoting to the workouts and accompanying preparations.

The only reason I didn't quit was that I realized I was in the worst possible position to make the decision. The greatest benefits of quitting were short-term, which is a sure sign of a mistake. I had emotional firsthand experience with the downsides of working out, but hadn't waited long enough to enjoy the benefits. I was also in the very beginning of the habit where it takes the most willpower, and is therefore the most mentally challenging.

So I persevered and gained fifteen pounds of muscle over two months, far and away the biggest gain I'd ever experienced. From that perspective, looking back, it was an obviously good decision to continue. Viscerally, it didn't feel that way at the time.

I still don't love working out, and there are negative aspects to it, but I no longer want to quit, as the benefits outweigh the costs. Even so, it's only now that I can seriously evaluate quitting with a level head. I can't imagine any specific event that would prompt me to do so, but I'd begrudgingly do it if I felt that whatever would take its place would be better in the long run.

A couple years before beginning weightlifting, I switched from being a vegan to a meat eater. I had been vegan for three years, really enjoyed it, and didn't want to quit. One of my habits is to expose myself to ideas I don't naturally agree with, and through that process I came to believe that eating well-raised meat was at least as healthy as a good vegan diet, if not healthier. From experience, I also knew that it would make traveling slightly more convenient to have a broader diet. (For an excellent book by my favorite thinker on food, read Death by Food Pyramid by Denise Minger)

I didn't want to start eating meat, but I did it anyway because I felt that it would be the best choice for me.

Now I'm glad I did it, but I would still happily switch back if I felt that the bulk of the evidence pointed towards a vegan diet for maximum health, and that the incremental health benefit was worth the decrease in travel convenience.

One of the biggest pitfalls in habit-building is quitting at the worst possible time, accruing the fewest benefits for the most effort, while evaluating the situation from the cloudiest perspective. Wait until you have loaded the habit, like it, and can think clearly. Of course, you should always use common sense. If a habit was tangibly harming your health, for example, you'd be right to quit as soon as you realized that.

Beware of Disruptors

Just as building positive habits creates a meta-benefit of becoming better at creating habits, certain negative habits will reach beyond their own scope and interfere negatively with other habits. If you have these habits, attack them first by finding their triggers and reprogramming them with new positive habits. By doing this you get a triple win: the elimination of the negative habit, the elimination of its tangential harm, and the creation of a new positive habit.

The three main disruptive habits are the use of drugs, the seeking of stimulation, and the habit of hanging out with negative friends.

Drugs and alcohol are vicious not only because they alter your ability to make good decisions, but also because they serve as triggers for themselves and other bad habits. A normal interruption to a habit can be course-corrected, but drugs and alcohol often lead to more drugs and alcohol, which further reduce your ability to make good decisions and stick with your positive habits.

Those who have a problem with seeking stimulation are never content focusing on one thing. Instead they jump from one to the next, trying to get a quick hit of dopamine. To build good habits, you must be able to focus on the process of what you're doing, both for personal satisfaction, and as a mechanism for improving your habits. An addiction to stimulation makes that impossible, and traps you in a cycle of web browsing, channel surfing, or simply focus-shifting.

Last, negative friends can be a huge hindrance to building positive habits. Often times friends see a friend, who was previously very similar to them and is now making changes, as a threat. They reason that if he wasn't happy with how he was, and they're like how he was, he must have a problem with them. This is not necessarily a sound train of thought, but the emotional impact is real.

If friends discourage the new habits you're building, it's your responsibility to deduce the root cause of their discouragement. Is it because they have domain knowledge of the changes you're trying to make and have legitimate concerns, or is it a product of insecurity?

Like essentially every problem in life, these disruptors can be dealt with through habits. You can replace drug and alcohol habits by finding their triggers and using them to trigger new positive habits. Use the impulse to seek stimulation as a trigger for a habit of taking a moment to think about what you should actually be doing with your time.

I don't recommend ditching all of your old friends just because you're making a change, but you could certainly create habits to surround yourself with positive people. The way I did this was to create a habit of only hanging out with people who I wanted to become better friends with. Within half a year this changed my social circle significantly for the better.

The Natural Habitat of A Habit Builder

For most activities, there is an ideal environment in which they take place. A weightlifter can get a decent workout in using his own bodyweight and items he finds around him, but to maximize his gains, he'll want to be in a well-equipped gym. A chef can whip up a good meal with leftovers over a single burner, but a stocked kitchen will allow him to cook better food in the same amount of time.

There is also an ideal habitat for a habit builder, but it relies less on physical tools and more on environment. This doesn't mean that building the ideal environment is any less important for the habit builder. Given the same level of willpower and motivation, having the right environment decreases slip-ups and reduces the stress of building habits.

Simplicity and freedom from distraction are the core

components of the habit builder's habitat. Building habits takes conscious focus, and to focus you must eliminate distractions. In particular, you want to eliminate the type of distractions that force you to use willpower. For example, watching advertisements might prompt you to weigh the pros and cons of buying something you don't really need. That mental battle, subconscious though it may be, reduces the willpower you have available for your habits.

Having junk food around, even if eating healthy isn't one of your active goals, will also decrease your willpower. Your brain is taxed not only by the sugar and cheap fats in the food, but also by negotiations with yourself on whether or not to eat the food.

A big part of our environment, one that isn't always looked at critically, is our peer group. Having friends who support you as you rebuild your habits is a major advantage. Having friends who are also motivated and building habits to help them reach their goals is doubly good.

On the other hand, friends who are threatened by your proactivity or are closed minded to anything outside their immediate comfort zone will become a huge drag on your progress. If they argue with you, tease you, or try to chip away at your progress, you will be slowed down. If they introduce any doubt in your own mind, you again have to use willpower to push yourself to do habits that could otherwise be easy to adopt.

Most of your focus should be directly on the habits you're

trying to build. There's no better angle to hit a nail than head-on. Be aware of your environment, though, and make changes to improve it. Short-term efforts to improve your environment can pay off big in the long term by making new habits easier and faster to build.

Imposing Your Habits on Others

Whenever I adopt a new habit, I have the urge to share it with everyone I know and try to get them to switch to it. I used to act on this urge, but I've grown to believe that it was a mistake.

Real change is the product of motivation, either prompted by a problem in life or through analysis of one's goals. When you adopt a new habit and try to convince others to do the same, they're skipping the stage of discovering or building that motivation. Without it, they'll give up when the going gets tough, feel bad about it, possibly resent you for succeeding at it, and be ever so slightly less inclined to create other new habits. By trying to help them, you may be doing them a disservice.

On the other hand, quietly building habits on your own without pushing them on your friends will expose them to new tools that they can use in their own lives when the time is right. If you eat healthy food and your friend eventually decides that they need to get in shape, they'll come to you for advice when their motivation is high enough.

The only time it's likely to be helpful to suggest a habit to a friend is when he asks for help or advice on a problem you've solved through habits. At that point you're sharing with him, not pushing. He's built the motivation, and may be ready to see a habit through to completion. You can even offer to keep him accountable.

PRACTICAL ANALYSIS OF VARIOUS HABITS

We've talked abstractly about habits first because the ultimate goal is for you to be able to identify an area you'd like to improve in, design a habit to fix it, and implement that habit. In addition, as an avid practitioner of habit-building, I've got a lot of specific advice on common habits that people endeavor to build.

You can read this section straight through to get ideas for new habits to create, you can read specific habits that appeal to you, or you can save it for later as a reference when you happen to be tackling a habit that I've gone through before.

Most of these habits are current habits, and all of them are habits I've done successfully with good results at some point. All practice, no unsubstantiated theory.

For each habit, I will include pros and cons of integrating the habit, an evaluation of the difficulty, the general path I'd suggest to take, and in some cases, general notes on the habit. Because habits are so personal, all of these factors will be different for you. You can use my experience as a rough guideline, knowing that these habits are possible to build, and perhaps utilizing a few pointers to help you along the way.

Positivity Habits

People accept work and productivity habits as givens, but few people think of general outlook as something that is controlled by habit. Outlook is influenced by external events, but is by definition your reaction to those events. By creating positive habits around how you react to external events, you improve your outlook.

This sounds like new age hogwash, but it is real and has a profound effect. The result is that it feels like nothing bad ever happens to you. I can objectively think of negative things that happen to me, but my immediate instinct is now to think, "Yeah, but that's not so bad. And besides, this other good thing happened to me."

Positivity Towards Yourself

Building positivity towards yourself is the process of drastically increasing the portion of your time you consider yourself to be happy, minimizing the emotional toll of "bad" events, and maintaining an even, positive mood. The effect of this habit is huge compared to the amount of effort it takes, making it a pretty easy choice for just about anyone.

Pros:
- Increased optimism
- Increased ability to deal with negative events
- Improved mood which is conducive to better relationships

Cons:

- Some people identify with negativity and feel like becoming positive is losing part of their identity
- Negative friends may find you more difficult to relate to

Path:

Becoming positive is a one-habit job that takes one to three months. You will notice a difference after one month, but it will have built so gradually that you may discount it's effectiveness. This is similar to having laser eye surgery, where after a couple months you can't remember having bad vision, and the wonder of perfect eyesight no longer seems so amazing.

From now on, every time you have any negative thought, simply think of one positive aspect of the situation. The positive aspect doesn't have to be equal in magnitude to the negative aspects, it just has to exist.

For example: if your car gets towed, you can think about how now you'll get credit card miles when you pay for the tow. If your dog dies, you might think about how you never have to feed it anymore. If your girlfriend breaks up with you, you can think about how you've just increased the chances that you'll end up with someone even better.

There's no need to dwell on the positive, use it to rationalize the negative, or anything like that. Just search for it, find it, and move on.

Notes:

At first this process will feel cumbersome and unwieldy, which will discourage you from continuing with the habit. Remember that if you've committed to this habit, you should not quit in the loading phase where there are no benefits but there is effort required.

After a period of two to four weeks, the habit will become almost automatic. Remain vigilant and make sure that you're still doing it. After two or three months you will have trained your brain to automatically come up with the positives.

This habit builds the skill of seeing the positives in things and makes it happen automatically. Our knee-jerk reaction to bad events can be to only see, and to dwell on, the negative, giving us a biased view that can affect our mood and paralyze us from acting. By seeing the positive automatically, we remain even-keeled and are even able to remain positive even in the face of negative events.

In my experience, this habit doesn't require much maintenance. I did it for three months, and ten years later am still optimistic and happy all of the time.

Positivity Towards Others

It's a shame that everyone else is an idiot. Dealing with such stupidity on a daily basis can make us resent others, feel superior, and interact with others in suboptimal ways.

Of course, it's important to remember that to everyone else, we're the idiots. I recently had an argument with a cruise ship staff member about how their system failed and overcharged me significantly for internet usage. Halfway through the argument I realized that both of us were certain that we were in the right, and equally certain that the other person was a complete idiot.

Despite such strong convictions on both of our sides, and regardless of who was right in that one situation, it's impossible that either of us is actually the non-idiot in every encounter we have. In the face of that uncertainty of never truly knowing whether one is right or wrong, the best we can do is to have compassion towards the other person and acknowledge the paradox of being certain in our position yet aware that our strong convictions are sometimes wrong.

Whether other people are doing smart things, dumb things, things that help us, or things that harm us, both parties can be best served through fostering compassion and minimizing focus on how wrong the other is.

Pros:
- Increased ability to work with strangers and acquaintances
- Increased feeling of goodwill towards others
- Increased openness and willingness to be positively influenced
- Increased opportunity to consider more expansive view of situations

Cons:
- In some situations you need to be insistent and assertive or your complaint won't be taken

seriously. Increasing compassion can make it more difficult to do this.

Path:

I used to eat at this hippie restaurant in Austin, Texas that served incredible macrobiotic food. They had a single bathroom, which sometimes had a line. While waiting in line for the bathroom, there was a bulletin board on which anyone could post a business card or flyer. Most of the flyers were touting various new-age examples of snake oil, but there was one that wasn't selling anything and just had a few sentences on it.

"Remember that everyone is just doing their best and trying to be happy, just like you."

Just like the self-happiness habit, you can use that idea to shift your perspective on other people. Whenever you find yourself thinking poorly of someone or in some sort of conflict with someone, force yourself to say to yourself, "Remember that this person is just doing their best and trying to be happy, just like me."

I found that this one took longer to internalize than the previous habit of being happy all of the time. My guess is that as an introvert who works alone, I don't have enough opportunities for minor conflict or frustration with others to fully implement the habit quickly. Even after a couple years, I'm still semi-consciously reminding myself to do this, but it helps every time.

Notes:

This habit feels sort of silly, but for me at least, I find that it instantly shifts my perception, and I am able to see my counterpart as a real human being, for whom any given interaction is a tiny slice of their life. That puts things in context and all of a sudden I'm able to find reasonable justifications for their behavior.

In the case of the internet usage argument, I could image how this girl who was helping me wasn't properly trained, and was doing her best. I thought about how frustrating it must be for her to field internet-related queries from angry people who know even less about the internet than she does. Last, I thought about how it must be stressful for her to work on a cruise ship all the time, compared to the stress-free experience I had as a passenger.

One of my personal weaknesses is a lack of empathy, so this habit may be more effective for me than for others. If you feel like you don't get frustrated with others often and can usually see their point of view, your time may be better spent on other habits.

Health Habits

Health habits are some of my favorites to work on because they have extraordinarily high payoffs. Rather than improve just one area of your life, they tend to really transfer well to other areas. Unless you already have an excellent repertoire of health habits, I'd encourage you to start with a health habit or two.

I use health as a general term to describe habits which will improve your life expectancy, average well-being, as well as your ability to use your physical and mental facilities to their maximum. Each habit will specialize along one or two of those axes, but each should have some positive impact on all of them.

Eating Healthy Food

Eating healthy food may be the single most important habit that you can cultivate. It has a large impact on life expectancy, well-being, and the use of your faculties. The most surprising improvement is the increase to mood and mental ability not normally associated with healthy eating.

In addition, eating healthy food encourages an upward spiral of taking good care of oneself, feeling better because of it, and, as a result, being motivated to build other positive habits. Commonly you'll see people begin to eat healthy, and then find that their motivation to use drugs or drink decreases, while their motivation to exercise increases.

My motivation for eating healthy changed when I read the book, Live Long Enough to Live Forever by Ray Kurzweil. Besides laying out a reasonable and sustainable diet, he also explained the precise negative implications of eating unhealthy food. When I understood the long term negative effects of continuing to rebel and eat McDonalds, sweets, and fried food, I immediately began a habit of eating healthily, which has persisted to today.

Pros:

- Longer lifespan
- Higher quality of life
- No brain fog
- Increased motivation for other healthy habits
- Fewer illnesses

Cons:

- Decreased convenience, especially while traveling
- Possible resentment among family and friends who do not eat healthy
- Challenging adjustment period

Path:

There are various specific diets that are very healthy and will serve you well. You can be vegan, lacto-vegetarian, pescatarian, or omnivore and have a healthy diet. Reasonable arguments for and against any of these specific diets can be made, but there are so many contradictory opinions that it's unlikely that any of those diets, under ideal circumstances, is better or worse than any other.

On the other hand, there are a few key dietary components that are universally, or near-universally, agreed to be significant. Rather than get caught of in the dogma of any specific "named diet", it's better to focus on the few things that matter most.

Sugar and highly-refined grains are the most significantly unhealthy things in the standard diet. Eliminating those two groups of foods is about eighty percent of getting to a healthy diet. Focus your willpower getting them out of your diet.

Items to cut out include refined sugars (including all fruit juices), agave and maple syrups, and honey, and refined grains such as white flour, white rice, and white pasta. You'll be inclined to find cheats like "whole wheat" bread whose main ingredient is actually white flour, but it's important to avoid those.

These simple processed carbohydrates are physically and mentally addictive. It is best to quit cold turkey. The first year is difficult, but then it becomes very easy. By then, you will have completely weaned yourself off of them, you will find them to be too sweet and unpleasant, and your honest preference will be for healthier foods. That's how you build a long-term healthy diet.

It's important that you replace these foods with new foods. Just cutting them out will leave you at a caloric deficit, which your body will fight by introducing cravings. I would recommend eating more foods that you like, even if they're not the healthiest. Replacing French fries with plain kale will be tough, but replacing them with baked sweet potatoes is pretty easy. In particular, increase your intake of complex carbohydrates, like brown rice, as well as natural simple carbohydrates like fruit.

The goal isn't to have a perfect diet in every way, but to eliminate the dozen or so foods that do the most damage, and to enjoy your diet enough to make it sustainable. Food is such a fundamental part of life that you cannot rely on willpower in the long term. Rely on it in the short term to create the habit, and then enjoy your new preferences for healthy food.

Notes:

This habit may sound impossible to some people, which will prevent them from even trying it. It's important to remember that the deprivation only lasts for a short time relative to one's life span and is then followed by an eternity of automatic healthy eating.

Once you enter the maintenance phase, you can allow yourself to eat unhealthy food under certain circumstances. My personal rule is to adhere one-hundred percent to healthy eating while at home, and to eat whatever is convenient while traveling. As a pattern I find that for the first week of traveling I gravitate towards unhealthy foods, but then start wanting to eat the healthiest stuff available, and can't wait to return to my perfect diet back home.

When you successfully tackle sugar and refined carbohydrates, you can turn your attention to fats. The greatest threat is consuming too many Omega-6 and Omega-9 fats. These are found in most cooking oils as well as non-pasture raised meat, eggs, and dairy. For the next wave, limit your oil intake to coconut oil for cooking and dressing, olive oil for dressing, and grass-fed butter. Meat should be limited to grass-fed beef and lamb, pasture-raised pork and poultry and wild-caught fish.

Because limiting processed carbohydrates is so important, I would focus on it exclusively rather than trying to do oils and fats at the same time. Success for that first habit is critical enough to warrant eating unhealthy oils in the process.

When adding new foods into your diet to replace the unhealthy ones, experiment with extremely healthy foods like miso soup, kale, cruciferous vegetables, tempeh, nuts, and seeds. Don't force yourself to eat them if you don't like them, but keep an eye out for those that do appeal to you.

The hardest part of adhering to a new diet is taking the time and effort to find something healthy to eat when you are starving and/or tired. It's easy to have willpower when a beautiful spread of healthy food is laid out in front of you, but it's a lot harder when every option readily available to you is full of sugar or white flour, and you'd have to go to great lengths to get something decent.

The best remedy is to plan every one of your meals in advance. This is challenging to do, but the effort virtually guarantees success. Have a default meal for breakfast, lunch, and dinner for which you always have ingredients on hand. For example, I eat a sardine sandwich and tuna sandwich almost every day for lunch. Any time I'm running low on Ezekiel bread, spinach, hummus, or fish, I restock so that I'm never more than a few minutes away from a healthy meal.

Good Sleep

Good sleep feels like a luxury and a superpower at the same time. Sleeping as long as you want to and waking up without an alarm clock smacks of being on vacation, but being alert and working at your peak when others are dragging and relying on coffee makes you feel invincible.

The goal with good sleep is to get as much sleep as your body wants, probably around 8 hours on average, and to wake up without an alarm clock.

A long-term view is critical when attacking the sleep habit. In any given week, you can sacrifice your sleep for more time spent working, and possibly even more high-quality output. But over the long term, you'll find that the quantity of quality output you are able to produce will be directly correlated to how closely you are able to follow your body's natural sleep patterns.

Pros:
- Higher energy levels
- Less stress
- Improved focus
- Improved mental abilities
- Less susceptibility to depression

Cons:

- Less awake hours to allocate
- Possible buffer time that is hard to use optimally

Path:

The first step towards a good sleep habit is creating a good sleep environment. The key components of a good sleep environment are complete darkness and silence.

If you can completely darken your bedroom, this is the best option. You can get heavy-duty blackout curtains, turn off the lights outside your door, cover every LED on your electronics, and remove any nightlights. This is ideal, but not always practical, especially if you share your bedroom with someone with slightly less zeal for habit-building.

The next best option is to buy a sleep mask. I've tried many of them and found the inexpensive Bucky 40 Blinks mask to be the best. It's good right off the bat, but as you use it more it will soften and become even more comfortable. It's important to wear the mask every single night, even though you will just pull it off in your sleep for the first few weeks. The only way to get past that is to wear it even though you know it won't last the night.

If you live in a very quiet environment, you may not need earplugs. If you do need earplugs, the best ones you can buy are the Hearo 33db earplugs. They're very comfortable, block as much or more sound than every other earplug, and are cheap enough that you can keep a bunch on hand and a few in your travel bag. Although it's best to not use an alarm clock long-term, you'll be able to hear it through the earplugs.

You may think that you only need four or six hours of sleep, because that's how long you naturally wake up after, but that is likely to change once you have a good sleep environment. Most people need around eight.

Rather than regulate your wake up time, regulate your bedtime. This will give your body the consistency to build a sleep schedule that is optimal for you. If you must be up at a certain time, which is true for most of us, set an alarm for that time, but go to sleep nine hours before the alarm will go off. If you find that you are consistently sleeping until the alarm goes off, move your bedtime back even further. That probably means that you are rather sleep-deprived and your body is catching up. Even if you sleep ten hours a night for a couple weeks, you should pull back to around eight hours per night.

Light, particularly the blue light from screens, tells the pineal gland in our brains that it's still daytime. If you have trouble falling asleep, as I used to, it may be because you're exposing yourself to screens up until the time you try to go to sleep.

In addition to your bedtime, set a strict screens-off time one or two hours prior to your bedtime. This is a great time to do some daily reading. A kindle on a very low brightness setting, or illuminated with a normal incandescent or LED light, will not disrupt your sleep schedule.

Adjusting will take a few weeks, but you'll soon feel better than you ever have, and be totally unwilling to switch back to your old schedule. You'll probably find that you naturally fall asleep shortly before your actual bedtime (unless you're reading a great book), and that your wakeup times will vary by an hour or so, but will average around eight hours. That time in the morning is great for activities that don't have to happen every single day, like doing laundry, organizing, and catching up on email. If you sleep through it, it's better to push the activities to the next day and enjoy the sleep your body needs.

Notes:

You may want to record how much sleep you get every day. When I first switched to this schedule over a year ago, I was convinced that I was sleeping nine or ten hours every night. However, when I averaged it out, it was almost exactly eight hours. The variance was my body's natural reaction to intense days and relaxing days.

The optimal sleep temperature is around sixty-five degrees. I've experimented with this and haven't found it to have any noticeable impact on my sleep, but you may want to try it as well.

Meditation

I've never been naturally drawn to meditation. It always seemed too wishy-washy and time consuming. Over time I noticed that many of the people I respected most cited meditation as one of the most important things that they did. This sounded ridiculous to me, but given the overwhelmingly high quality of advice I got from them apart from meditation, I finally opened up to it.

The tipping point for me was reading the excellent book, the Willpower Instinct, which said that the two best practices for increasing willpower were working out and meditating every day. I gave it a shot, waited the two months they claimed it would take to get the benefits, and haven't looked back since.

There are a lot of purported benefits of meditation, all of which I'm sure are experienced by one person or another, but the most significant benefit I've derived is better impulse control. Friends who also meditate report similar significant increases.

Pros:
- Improved impulse control
- Less stress
- Improved focus

Cons:
- Requires quiet area, which can be hard to find
- Benefits beyond impulse control may vary by person

Path:

If you meditate for five minutes a day, you will notice results within two months. That's the claim the Willpower Instinct book made, and it mirrored my experience. If you enjoy meditating, you can do it for longer, and if you absolutely hate it, you can start with less time and build up.

Every day, just sit for five minutes in a quiet space, close your eyes, and focus on your breath. For the first minute or two, it can help to subvocalize, "breathe in.... breathe out... breathe in... breathe out..." Such a simple task is enough to keep your mind focused.

Your overriding goal is just to sit there for five minutes. Any time you do that, you have successfully meditated. When you notice that your mind starts thinking about something else, refocus on your breath.

The loading period for meditating is approximately two months. After that you continue to meditate every single day, but you will slowly begin to see the benefits, which makes it much easier.

Notes:

A key distinction that made meditation easier for me was to realize that being really bad at it was a good thing. For one, it meant that I needed it, because I was unable to silence my mind, and second it meant that I was actually able to practice focusing my mind. If meditation were easy, I learned, it would not be as beneficial.

If you focus on the outcome of executing a perfect meditation session without your mind wandering once, you will get frustrated and want to quit. As always, focus on the process and count it as a win any time you sit with your eyes closed, trying your best, for five minutes.

The most tangible benefit I noticed from meditation was that it created a space in between feeling an impulse and acting on it. This sounds vague, but once you experience it, you will know exactly what I mean. Before, I could be working, and without a single conscious thought, I'd be browsing Facebook, thinking about how I should get back to work.

Now I catch myself every time and I consciously think, "Oh, I'm getting distracted and I'm about to click over to Facebook." I'll still give in sometimes and browse for a couple minutes, but I always notice the impulse, and often counteract it. Having this ability has helped me become more aware of triggers for distraction and has helped me stop being such a slave to subconscious impulses.

I also believe that it has helped me be satisfied and relaxed in otherwise annoying situations like waiting in line or dealing with bureaucracy, but I can't be completely sure meditation is the cause of this. At the very least, it's probably a contributing factor.

Drinking Tea Daily

I hesitate to include the daily tea habit because it is unequivocally less important than any other habit in this section. While the other habits could become core pieces of a huge change in lifestyle, drinking tea daily is just a "nice thing to do".

The reason I include it at all is because it's one of my

favorite habits. I started out hating tea, likening it to a cup of bath water, but it has now become part of my daily morning ritual to such a degree that I bring tea with me when I travel.

Besides the potential health benefits, a daily pot of tea creates a nice space to reflect and plan, and gives a calm and enduring energy different than that obtained from coffee or soda.

Pros:
- A relaxed time to think and plan
- Possible anti-cancer properties due to high antioxidants
- Consistent, focused energy from caffeine

Cons:
- Not as high impact as other habits
- Takes time
- Might turn you into a tea snob like me

Path:

While it's normal to drink fairly high-quality coffee, most people have never actually had good tea. The tea that's sold in small paper bags is terrible quality, often augmented with spray-on artificial flavor, and delivered in insufficient quality to brew properly.

To drink bagged tea and decide you don't like tea is to eat a beef-flavored dog snack and decide you don't like steak.

Start with a high-quality unflavored looseleaf tea. Green

tea or Genmaicha, green tea with toasted brown rice, are both excellent first choices. My favorite tea vendor is Samovar, whose teas are consistently good and high quality, but you can also find passable choices from Adagio that are a cheaper entry into tea.

Using a tea pot, water heated to the correct temperature (165 F or so for green tea), and a large tea-infusing basket, steep your tea for the prescribed amount of time (a minute and a half or so for green), and decant into a tea cup to drink.

Do this every day, even if you don't like tea at first. I went over the top and drank eight cups per day until I liked it, which only took about a week.

Notes:
One of my favorite aspects about tea is the space it creates for relaxation and reflection. If you don't feel that at first and just chug your tea, don't worry about it. I find that the more you drink tea, the more you appreciate it, and the slower you drink it to maximally enjoy it. Through that process you will naturally find the right pace.

If you'd like some variety, you can move on to puerh teas, which are darker and more similar to coffee, or to oolongs. Both of those types of tea can be brewed many times and can last an hour or more of repeated steepings. If you love green tea, but want something new, try a light Taiwanese oolong.

Vitamin D

The majority of Americans are deficient in vitamin D, which is an important vitamin for everything from your immune system to the strength of your bones and muscles. If you work indoors and don't spend an obviously significant amount of time in the sun every day or two, you are almost certainly deficient.

To find out, you can get an inexpensive (around $50) test and get your results in just a couple days. I already knew that I was probably deficient before getting the test, but actually seeing low numbers on paper was what finally spurred me to action to take vitamin D every day.

Pros:
- Stronger immune system
- Easier to build muscle
- Stronger bones

Cons:
- None

Path:

Take 10,000iu per day until you are no longer deficient (or after 30 days if you don't get another test to check). Then drop down to 5,000iu.

Notes:
I'm not a doctor, but this has worked for me and others. I am extremely averse to swallowing pills, and in fact have never swallowed a pill besides these vitamin D pills. However, research very strongly suggests that vitamin D

is completely safe and without side effects or downsides. As with anything you introduce to your body, it's not a bad idea to check with your doctor.

Working Out

Working out is one of those habits that can be annoying to do at the time, but you quickly become so acclimatized to its benefits that you become very reluctant to ever quit it. If you're already very physically active in your life, you're likely already receiving the benefits of working out, and can skip this one. But if you tend to spent most of your life without much activity, this should be a high priority.

Pros:
- Increased longevity
- Better sleep
- Improved body composition
- Improved self-esteem
- Increased physical abilities

Cons:
- Impacts your schedule significantly
- Some workouts leave you temporarily depleted of energy

Path:
I'm not an expert on working out, but Dick Talens is. He's the co-founder of Fitocracy and has successfully trained the full spectrum of clients, ranging from Miss America, to me. In the past I had tried a variety of methods to try to gain lean mass, and had little or no success. He claimed

that he could give me a program that would minimize time in the gym and maximize my gains. In two months I gained fifteen pounds of lean mass.

Dick's system works for men and women, whether trying to lose or gain weight. You can work with him, or another trainer, to get a perfectly tailored program, but I will outline the basics here so that you can do it on your own.

Work out three days a week, doing three exercises each day. Monday is deadlifts, pullups, and rows. Wednesday is bench press, incline bench press, and curls. Friday is squat or leg press, straight-leg deadlift, and cable crunches. Deadlifts of both varieties are two sets of 4-6 reps, pullups are three sets of 4-6, everything else is three sets of 8-12.

After a couple warmup sets of 50% and 75% of your maximum weight, do your maximum. Then drop the weight by ten percent and do the same number of reps as before, plus one. If you have a third set, drop by another ten percent and increase by one more rep. For pullups, if you can do at least 4 with just your body weight, you add weight to the first one.

If you hit the maximum in the range the previous week, you increase the weight by five or ten pounds and reset to the bottom of the range. So if you bench pressed 100 at twelve reps last week, do 110 at eight this week.

Notes:

This is a general formula that will get good results for anyone. You can customize it and pair it with an effective diet to get even more out of your time. Whatever you do, don't jump from plan to plan, without giving any one the time it needs to get results. In my experience it takes three to four weeks to notice anything, and 8 weeks to notice a profound difference.

Shifting your diet to 30-40% protein, including a shake one hour before working out, will help. If you want to gain or lose weight, you need to count your calories carefully and then increase or decrease by about five-hundred calories per day to gain or lose, respectively. That surplus or deficit will cause one pound of gain or loss per week. As long as you eat enough protein, it will mostly be fat that is lost.

If you don't know how to do the exercises mentioned above, you can watch Youtube videos to learn. Or if you want to dive deep, read the excellent book Starting Strength by Mark Rippetoe.

Expansion Habits

We can think of everything we do during our lives as either input or output. Either we're creating something new or we're taking in outside influence. There is, of course, a direct correlation between these two things. Ideas don't exist in a vacuum, so whatever outside influences we're exposed to become a part of our creation process and affect our output.

For this reason, it's worth some time optimizing our input through habits, as well as our output. This chapter is full of habits that help increase the quality of input we take in, and use that input as constructively as possible.

Traveling to Unusual Countries

There is a difference between going on a vacation and traveling. One is an escape from reality, and the other is a means to connect more deeply with it. Travel allows us to see firsthand how other people live, think, and create. Without traveling we limit our view of the world to a rather narrow one. Creative excellence can come from such a narrow view, but not as easily is it can come from worldly experience and understanding.

Traveling is also a lot less expensive than vacation, because you are able to live more like locals live. Rather than trumped up resort charges, tour buses, and expensive touristy meals, you rent a local apartment, take public transportation, and eat where locals eat.

Pros:

- Exposure to vastly different mindsets
- Exposure to art, architecture, and nature outside your country
- Increased self-reliance

Cons:
- Can interfere with work unless you develop good travel work habits
- Can be expensive

Path:

Make a goal of a certain number of new places to visit per year, block out the time for it way in advance, and book at least one part of the trip early enough to commit to it.

When choosing the places to go, choose places that are radically different from those with which you're familiar. For example, Japan is a great choice because it's very different from everywhere else, can be traveled cheaply, and has a lot of culture and beauty to offer. It was one of the first places I traveled to, and even after a dozen or so visits, it still surprises me every time.

In general, Europe and North America are similar enough that I wouldn't recommend choosing one as your expansionary place to visit if you live in the other one. That's not to say that you wouldn't have a great time visiting, just that it might not yield as much interesting and useful experience as somewhere more different like Asia, Africa, or South America.

If you're on a tight budget, just pick places that are closer to you. Even if you're just taking a road trip a couple states over, you're building the habit that will expand as you become able to travel to more places.

Notes:

I call traveling a habit because I've noticed that those who do it regularly get more out of it, go to more adventurous places, and continue as they get older. But, just like other habits, it seems that many people lose their sense of adventure as they get older and stop visiting new places. It doesn't have to be that way, though– I've met dozens of older people in some of the most unusual places I've visited.

There is also a lot of value in going back to places you've already visited, rather than constantly going to new places. I personally like a 50/50 distribution, but as long as there are some new places in the mix, I think any ratio is fine.

I've written another book entirely about traveling in an expansionary manner. It's called Life Nomadic and is available on Kindle and in paperback on Amazon.

Writing Daily

I began writing my blog nine years ago, completely on a lark and without any expectations for it. Since then it's become a major avenue of connecting with other people, and has become a primary source of income, but the biggest benefit is that it has made me a clearer and more precise thinker and communicator. For that reason, I recommend that you build the habit of writing daily as well.

Pros:
- Clearer thinking
- Better communication skills
- Historic log of thoughts and events

Cons:
- Time consuming at first

Path:

Write a prescribed amount every day. I find it easiest to assign myself to write a single blog post every day, but you could also choose a word count. When I'm writing a book I set my word count at 4000-7000 words per day, but 500 per day is plenty for blogging. If you plan on writing privately, you could go as low as 300 per day. You can also set a fixed amount of time. Half an hour of writing per day would be enough.

What you write about is not important. Neither is the quality of the writing. Constraining yourself to a topic or expecting a certain quality level will make the habit more difficult. Success is achieved if you sit down and write for the prescribed amount of time or number of words.

At first your writing might be horrible and you might find it difficult to articulate your thoughts. That's completely fine— it just means that you'll benefit even more from the habit. Over time the habit will become easy, you'll become very good at articulating your thoughts, and you'll end up becoming a decent writer.

Notes:

You'll get additional benefit from your habit if you post it to a blog. My habit is to write every day of the week and then post the best two to my blog. I've created a blogging platform called Sett which helps you get an audience for your writing, so if you create a free blog there you'll have in audience for your writing instantly.

If you're really stuck and want to break the habit, just write about how you're really stuck and want to break the habit. Even after nine years of writing, I still do this sometimes. As always, it's more important to focus on the process of maintaining the habit than the output which the habit creates.

To be clear, I recommend this habit even if you don't care at all about writing and don't want to blog or write a book. The real value is that it forces you to be thorough about evaluating thoughts, helps synthesize input into output, and transforms you into a clearer communicator.

Seek Out Masterpieces

This is a weird habit. I started it because I was working really hard and not leaving home for days on end. Worrying that I was living in an echo chamber and not getting enough outside influence, but unwilling to pull much time from work, I theorized that experiencing masterpieces would be a very efficient and concentrated way to get quality input.

It worked, but the greatest benefit I got was that being exposed to so many examples of mastery raised my own standards and was very inspiring. Even now that I'm not quite so cloistered with my work, I still continue this habit.

Pros:
- Exposure to mastery
- Increased motivation
- Increased personal standards

Cons:
- Could be a poor use of time if not in a location that has masterpieces accessible

Path:

Once per week, two weeks, or month, make the time to go see masterpieces. A masterpiece is anything made or performed by someone who is an expert in their craft. Obvious choices are art museums, symphony performances, and operas, but I'd extend the category to include stuff like factory tours of impressive companies.

For my own habit, I also include going into nature. Even though it's the product of natural evolution rather than mastery and creation, I find that it inspires me in the same way.

Notes:

I used to never go to art museums because I felt like I didn't know "how to appreciate art". Thanks to going on a couple tours from Museum Hack (the founder of which I'm now friends with), I learned that appreciating art doesn't require tons of knowledge or preparation. Just going to a museum, walking around for a couple hours and stopping if and when you find something that's interesting to you, is plenty.

Pushing Your Comfort Zone

Our brains are lazy and we're creatures of habit. That means that without conscious effort, we will only do what is comfortable and familiar. This is actually a good thing overall, and is the underpinning of how habits work. By making desirable behaviors comfortable and familiar, we can change them from being cumbersome and mentally taxing to comfortable and easy.

The downside of our inclination towards remaining in our comfort zone is that we can become too accustomed to it and pass up opportunities to grow and experience new things in ways which would inspire and change us. For that reason, we need to prod ourselves regularly to do things that are starkly outside of our comfort zones.

Everyone faces fear when pushing out of their comfort zone, but fear alone is not a good reason to avoid doing something. In fact, those times when we are able to confront fear and push ourselves are often the times where we make breakthroughs in life.

Pros:

- Guarantees personal growth
- Builds confidence
- Helps discover new interests and abilities

Cons:
- Can be awkward and tedious

Path:

This habit works best with the specific trigger of thinking, "I'd like to do _____, but I'm too scared/nervous". For it to properly work, you must be able to be honest with yourself, as discussed earlier. Many people will convince themselves that they're not actually scared, they're just busy or not really interested, and will give themselves a pass.

Whenever you have that feeling of wanting to do something, but being too nervous, you should immediately think, "Okay, now I have to do it." Then, of course, you take the first step and go do it.

This habit is also a classic example of focusing on the process rather than the outcome. Let's say that you see an attractive woman you want to go talk to her. You may be scared, and would normally be inclined to chicken out, but you have set this habit and now you have to go do it. If you walk up to the woman, say hello, and she immediately tells you to leave her alone and walks away, you've completely succeeded. The success is in the process of expanding your comfort zone.

When loading this habit, you should do it every single

time you have the impulse not to. Only by doing that will you be able to expand your comfort zone when it's really difficult to do so. Over time, though, it's fair to think a bit more about why you want to do something, and make the judgment call if you should expand your comfort zone or not. However, if you find that you've stopped doing it, it might be time to revert to the loading habit of doing it every single time.

Notes:

This habit does not mean to follow every impulse you have, of course. There's a good reason that humans have impulse control. The best examples of cases where this habit comes into play are positive interactions with strangers and trying out new activities.

I am a natural introvert and grew up being very bad with women. Part of what I needed to do to improve myself in this area was to try to talk to every woman I was attracted to, even if I was scared half to death. Through that process I expanded my comfort zone and learned exponentially more than I could have if I had played it safe.

A more recent example was when a friend recommended that I try "Ecstatic Dance". It didn't sound like my sort of thing, but my friend who recommended it to me had a history of always giving good advice. Although it didn't sound like much fun to me, I was also aware that the main reason I didn't want to go was because I was terrified of showing up at this event, not knowing anyone or anything about it, and then dancing without reservation for four hours. As soon as I realized that I was scared to go, I knew that I had no other choice.

Ecstatic dance wasn't necessarily something I'd do again, but even if I had hated it, I would have been happy to have pushed myself out of my comfort zone and reinforced this habit.

Organization Habits

I'm not a naturally organized or tidy person. As a child, battles were fought over the cleanliness of my room, and when I moved out, I took a certain pride in not being too organized or tidy. It didn't matter, I thought.

However, over time I noticed that having a clean and uncluttered living and working space makes it easier to think, helps keep my stress levels low, and improves my mood. When I realized this, I created several habits that work together to make being tidy and organized easy.

Daily Imperfect Cleaning

Part of what kept my house messy was the magnitude of effort that it would take to get it fully clean. If the house was already pretty clean, and I was in just the right mood, I could put in a little time and get it perfect. If the house slipped into the messy territory, though, procrastination kicked in, and I would avoid doing the hard work for days or weeks, only to repeat the cycle again once cleaned.

The solution to the problem is to acknowledge that keeping your space perfectly clean is not worth the effort to you. Unless that changes, which is unlikely unless you're already executing on it, you will never keep your place perfectly clean all the time.

On the other hand, if you can set a lower standard for acceptable cleanliness, cleaning becomes a lot easier, and a lot of the pressure is relieved. I recommend setting this level at a nine out of ten, which is arbitrary but should be something that you can envision.

Pros:
- Less stress
- Easier to focus and think
- Less prep needed for guests

Cons:
- Takes time daily

Path:

Every day, you will clean your house to a "nine out of ten" standard twice. Choose specific triggers that happen every day at home, and use them to trigger the habit. For example, I do this every day when I finish my tea, and again when I turn my computer off for the night.

By choosing two times to clean, you make each cleaning very unimposing. Time yourself while you do it for the first few times. If you don't like cleaning, as I didn't, you'll be very surprised at just how quickly you can clean your house to this standard. Once you mentally accept how quick it is, it will be very easy to stick to the habit.

When choosing your cleaning times, make sure that you will not be tired or pressed for time when they occur. When integrating this habit myself, I found that if I was tired or busy, I was very inclined to skip a cleaning, thinking, "It's not that messy now– I can pick up the slack later." Of course, that's the beginning of the end.

Clearly define what your standard means. For me it means that everything I'm not going to use in the next 12 hours is stored in its place, no dishes are in the sink, and no surfaces are obviously dirty. It's important to be able to determine accurately whether you're done or not, otherwise the task can drag on into perfectionism and become too much of a burden to do twice a day.

Notes:

In addition to the two short cleaning times to a nine out of ten, you might add the additional requirement of doing one extra thing like vacuuming a room, scrubbing the sink, or washing the stove. If you do that, your space will end up being at a ten out of ten a lot of the time because you're doing fourteen additional tasks per week that often don't take a week to get dirty again.

The Easy Habit to Stay On Top of Email

There are a number of extremely complicated systems for staying on top of email. Most of them probably work, too, except that integrating a complex system into your life is difficult and is unlikely to actually become a habit before you give up on it.

Staying current with email doesn't have to be difficult. By breaking this task down to the simplest possible habit - deciding which email requires a reply - you can make email processing very simple.

Pros:
- Reply to important emails quickly

- Never lose or forget about emails

Cons:
- None

Path:

Most email clients, including the Gmail web interface and Thunderbird, have a mechanism for starring or flagging emails. As soon as you read any email that requires further action, including replying, following up, visiting a web site, etc., you flag or star it.

Once per day, preferably early afternoon when you've had the chance to read emails and still have a bunch of productive time left, go through all of the starred emails and either reply, take the necessary action, or unstar it.

Notes:

You can also reply to email immediately. Even if you're going to do this, star it first. This gets you into the habit of deciding up front if email is going to be acted on or not, which is the important part. The nice thing about this habit is that because the deciding is decoupled from the acting, there's never a good reason not to star. Then, even if you've skipped the writing phase for a few days, say while traveling, you can pick back up with all of your starred emails as soon as you have the time.

Keeping a Useful Calendar

The problem with trying to keep appointments and events

on a calendar is that unless every single one is on there, you can't rely on your calendar. If you can't rely on your calendar, then there's no point in actually keeping one, because it's taking up time and not relieving you of the mental load of having to keep track of things.

For that reason, the critical component of a useful calendar system is making sure that every single thing gets put on it. Only once you reach that state will having a calendar be more of a benefit than a burden.

Pros:
- Drastically reduces the chance of missing and being late to appointments
- Eliminates the need to keep mental track of appointments

Cons:
- Once you don't rely on your memory for your schedule, failure to put something on your calendar can result in you missing it and not even realizing it.

Path:

The key with a calendar, like emails, is focusing only on the first step and aiming for perfect adherence. Whenever you commit to do anything on any date, or are given a date that will be useful to you in the future, put it on your calendar on your phone. Later you can work on syncing with your laptop, but since you know you'll always have your phone on you, it's a good place to start.

When in doubt on whether or not you'll need a date in the future, put it down. Remember that you will only use your calendar if you trust it completely.

Notes:

In the beginning you won't actually use all of the entries on your calendar for anything, and this will feel like a waste of time. By now this shouldn't be much of a surprise— it's a very typical indicator that you're in the loading phase of a habit.

Once your brain trusts that your entire schedule is on your calendar, you will notice that you start referring to it more. This won't happen instantly, because we're not building a new habit; we're replacing the habit of trying to remember all dates in your head. Eventually, maybe a month or two after you're putting every single thing on your calendar, you'll start relying on it and trusting it.

If you travel a lot, look into using TripIt to handle all of the entries for flights, hotels, and rental cars. Since those are a huge portion of the things I put into my calendar, using TripIt reduces my input to my calendar by at least fifty percent.

Getting Rid of Stuff

This habit will be a bit more dogmatic than others, as I believe that having some semblance of minimalism in one's life is a good thing. This wasn't always the case, as I was a proud Accumulator of Stuff for most of my life. At one point I had a room in my house whose sole purpose was to warehouse all of the computers, parts, and other junk I had.

Since then I've come around to having as few possessions as possible. I still like my gear, but I find that having fewer possessions saves me from distraction and spending time tending to the possessions and allows me to focus where I spend money instead of having it seep out of my wallet from all directions.

The essential habit of becoming a minimalist is the habit of regularly evaluating how your possessions either add to or detract from the conscious life you're living and then getting rid of those things that are burdensome. If you build that habit, you will eventually find your life free of clutter.

Pros:
- Less clutter
- Recover money from stuff you've bought
- Easier to move and travel

Cons:
- Sometimes you will get rid of things that you actually could have used
- Takes time compared to just ignoring unused stuff

Path:

All around your house or apartment, you have stuff that you no longer use. The key to making this habit work is to understand that all of that stuff has negative value. Storing stuff that you won't actually use is worse than not having it at all. This is because it is a distraction, is depreciating, and may require maintenance, organization, and cost to store. If you understand that, you will have the motivation to get rid of it.

It's also important to understand that the true value of stuff is a combination of its utility to you and the present day amount that you can sell it for. The original price you paid, or the utility that you would get out of it in ideal (and unrealistic) conditions, is wholly irrelevant.

So if you paid $1000 for some amazing skis that would be fantastic if you still enjoyed skiing, but those skis can only be sold for $200, guess how much they're worth? Two hundred bucks. It hurts to admit this some time, but avoiding the truth never leads to it changing.

The getting rid of stuff habit should be triggered any time you see something that you haven't used in six to twelve months. When that happens, you should ask yourself whether you can get rid of it or not. If you're at least ninety percent sure that you could get rid of it, just do it.

Choose a spot in your house to move everything that you've decided to get rid of. A good spot would be your closet, where it's out of sight for most people, but where you'll see it regularly.

Whenever that pile gets big enough, get rid of everything in one big batch. Bring clothes to a thrift shop and take whatever they offer you. Donate whatever they won't take. Even if you get no money for the clothes you won't wear, it's better than having to sift through them every time you're picking out what you're going to wear.

The absolute easiest way to sell electronics is through Amazon. If you sign up for a seller account, you can send them a bulk box of everything that you don't want, and they will sell it alongside their own stuff. After fees I've found that this gets me approximately the same amount of money that selling individually on eBay does, but is way less of a hassle. Through the online interface you describe the condition of the item and set a price, and they do just about everything else. This works for anything that Amazon sells.

For big items like vehicles, appliances, and furniture, sell through craigslist. It's a hassle, but selling big things always is. You can make your life a lot easier by pricing things just a little bit on the low side. Remember that the goal isn't to become a professional used goods salesperson, it's to unclutter your life.

Notes:

When you don't get rid of things you aren't using, you are blinding yourself to a critical part of the consumer experience: what happens to things when you're done with them. When you have the habit of periodically getting rid of things you aren't using anymore, your brain begins to create links between the beginning (buying) and the end (selling) of all of your stuff.

This awareness of the full cycle will naturally make you a more value-conscious shopper, steering you away from items that are high price, low utility, and low lifetime value. On the other hand, you might find that certain categories of things (camera lenses, for example) retain their value well, and by selling them when you aren't using them anymore, you can actually afford to buy more of them.

Chances are that if you don't have this habit, and you have a mild inclination to hoard, as I do, you have a huge backlog of stuff that you could get rid of. Consider taking a Sunday and spending an hour or two hunting through your drawers, closets, boxes, garage, and attic, making a huge pile of everything that you have to get rid of. Then spend the rest of the day getting rid of it all.

If you have trouble finding the motivation for this habit, you could allow yourself to account for all of the money you get back from it separately, and use it for something that you wouldn't otherwise spend money on, like a trip. Long-term it's probably not best to connect a reward with the byproduct of overspending, but it can be a good way to get the ball rolling if necessary.

Social Habits

Good habits can benefit you in any area of your life, including areas like your social life, which you may not naturally think of as testbeds for new habits. However, like everything, the way you interact with people is largely based on a set of habits. By changing just a few of those habits, you can be a better friend, colleague, or family member.

Always Be On Time

It's easy to think of oneself as someone who is just always late, as if there's some sort of gene that gets expressed at birth to doom someone to never being on time. Moreover, it's easy to not really think of promptness, and to assume that since no one really makes a big issue of being fifteen minutes late to everything, that it's not actually a big deal.

The truth is that there are bigger deals than chronic tardiness, but it's such an easy habit to fix that you might as well do it. Overnight I went from being the type of person who was usually five to ten minutes late to the type of person who is exactly on time nearly every single time, and absolutely never seriously late.

The biggest change I noticed when I started being exactly on time to everything was that many people in my life started taking timeliness seriously. It's easier to do that when you know that the other person is going to be on time. You might think that by always being the person who is on time you end up waiting around for people.

This is true in the short term, but in the longer term everyone around you tends to be more on time, so there's less time wasted sitting around and waiting on both sides.

Pros:
- Give and receive more respect
- Less time waiting around
- Never miss opportunities because you were late
- Increased ability to estimate times

Cons:
- In the short term you end up waiting for people you know will be late

Path:

The bulk of success with this habit is building the proper motivation, and elevating timeliness from a nice bonus to an absolute imperative. This comes through understanding the benefits of being on time, as well as the idea that if you can't count on yourself to execute well on the simple and less important things, how can you count on yourself to execute on the big things? In other words, if you can't show up at a time you agreed on, how can you expect to do much more difficult things consistently?

The trick to always being on time is to show up everywhere five minutes early and wait around the corner until the exact right time. I usually check up on emails or read a few pages of a book on my phone. This sounds a little ridiculous, but the effect is magical: any time you say you will be somewhere at a certain time, you are there at that exact minute.

The five-minute buffer allows for a bit of bad estimation, traffic, parking, or other minutiae that people don't account for. Once you're maintaining the habit, you can cut that buffer down for routes you know really well. A big side benefit of this habit is that you always end up knowing what time you left and what time you arrived, so you learn how long it actually takes to get door-to-door from your place to various locations. That helps make estimates better in the future, and reinforces the habit of always being on time.

Notes:

This is one of those habits where it's key to focus on the process, not the outcome. In the beginning, especially if you have a reputation for being late, you will be waiting for people all the time. You'll show up on the dot, they'll assume you were going to be late, and so they'll be late. Take pride in the fact that you were exactly on time and read a book on your phone or something like that. Over time people will learn that you're always on time and will become much more punctual.

Delete or Contact

The set of tools we now have on the internet and on our phones makes it very easy to accumulate a large amount of contacts with whom we'll never actually follow up. This makes it easy to forget about people we actually wanted to keep in touch with and makes it a pain to scroll through a huge list of people just to find the person you want to text or call.

To fix this, we can create a habit that gets rid of people we're not going to get to know better, and simultaneously helps us stay in touch with people we care about.

Pros:
- Stay in touch with everyone you intend to
- Clean, organized phone book

Cons:
- Makes it confusing when a random person you've deleted texts you

Path:

Once a month, scroll through your entire phone book. For each person you haven't contacted in the past month, or since the last check, force yourself to either delete them from your phone or send them a message or make a call.

If you do this regularly, you can become one of those people who seems magically good at keeping in touch with everyone they meet. It also builds discipline to not ask for people's contact information if you won't actually contact them, because you get used to making that "delete or contact" decision.

Notes:

What this habit really does is help us act on decisions we've already made. Often we'll feel obligated to stay in touch with someone that we don't really want to, even though we know that we never will. Much better to just delete and move on, making space for people we actually would like to stay in touch with.

In addition to this habit, I routinely go through my Facebook friend list and delete people who I wouldn't want to go have dinner with. It's an arbitrary benchmark, but it makes it quick and easy to make decisions. I pruned my friend list down from almost two thousand friends to under two hundred, and Facebook is much more enjoyable to use, and is no longer a big distraction.

Productivity Habits

Productivity habits are some of the most powerful habits, because the way that we work tends to already be systematized to a certain extent. By tweaking and improving upon those systems, we can become incredibly effective executors, while simultaneously making that execution require much less willpower than before.
It's important to think of your job or your work primarily as a system of habits. Having a defined system allows you to pinpoint what's working and what isn't, and to iteratively improve it over time. Because you will most likely be spending the majority of your life being productive, working on these habits will become increasingly valuable over time.

The interesting effect of building productivity habits is that because so much of your output is defined by your habits, you'll have a major advantage in anything you do. So even if your specialty is programming, if you decide to become a writer, a lot of those habits that you built are universal enough that you'll start with a leg up.

You've probably heard the phrase, "if you want something done, give it to a busy person." That phrase makes sense because we know that busy people have, probably subconsciously, created habits to allow them to get a lot done. So much of getting things done is that system of habits, that their specialty doesn't really matter— just give them what needs to be done, and they'll do it.

This process is how you become the type of person who

is capable across many domains, and makes it look easy.

Twice, Then Quit

No matter how efficient or capable we are, we'll all run into days where we just don't want to work. Rather than pretend that this doesn't happen, or use it as an excuse to slack off, we can set the goal of getting the most possible work out of ourselves without wrecking future productivity.

This realistic view may not be as productive short-term as just burning ourselves out, but it does lead to higher long-term productivity, which should always be the time horizon upon which we grade ourselves.

The "Twice, Then Quit" method is a method that I first heard used in Zen meditation to help practitioners extend their meditation practices without burning out. I adapted it for work and found it to be very effective there as well.

Pros:
- Always gets more work done than just quitting
- Sometimes leads to breaking through barriers like "writer's block"
- Allows one to quit when appropriate without guilt

Cons:
- Not always the most effective method short-term
- Requires more willpower than just quitting

Path:
Twice, then Quit is very simple. When you want to quit

working for the first time, don't. Push through and work some more. The second time you want to quit, also don't quit. Push through again. The third time you want to quit, go ahead and quit.

This habit is deceptively simple, but is very effective. It allows us to push through while simultaneously taking pressure off because we know that there's a light at the end of the tunnel and that we won't drive ourselves to complete exhaustion.

It also allows us to quit when we are really exhausted, rather than when we hit a small stumbling block. Often I'll feel exhausted because the work ahead of me seems daunting, but once I push through for the first time, I get through a tough bit, and then feel like working again. So even when you don't actually push twice, but then quit, you'll benefit from the habit.

Last, when you finally do quit, you can enjoy your time or spend it working on something else, rather than feeling like you should have kept working. This is important, because we want to maximize all of the use of our time, not just the time we spend producing. When you push through twice but still want to quit, you can be confident that you gave it a solid effort and that you need a little bit of time off before tackling the problem again. That lack of ambiguity erases unnecessary guilt.

Notes:

The only major pitfall in this habit is that it's possible to use it as an excuse to quit when you really shouldn't.

Maybe you've been invited to do something fun, but you know you should really work, so you go through the motions of wanting to quit twice, and then you leave and go see the movie.

That would be a mistake. The trigger for twice, then quit, should be feeling exhausted, being unable to focus on the work at hand, or feeling like you're not able to muster the effort towards creating high-quality work.

Don't beat yourself up if you make the mistake of triggering the habit when you shouldn't— just try to be honest with yourself about the reasons and use that to inform future uses.

Eliminate Starting Procrastination

When I began trying to track down where wasted time was going, I found that I procrastinated quite a lot. That wasn't surprising by itself, but what I didn't expect to find was that almost all of my wasted time was before I even got to work.

It felt as though I would wake up, have a quick pot of tea, and then immediately get to work. In reality, I would wake up, have my cup of tea, and then browse the internet and engage in low-productivity activities almost until lunch time!

Rather than tackle procrastination in general, I decided that if I could just get myself to start work earlier, my problems would mostly go away. That turned out to be true, and the solution was simple and painless.

Pros:
- More potential hours of work per day
- Less wasted time

Cons:
- It's pleasant to waste a bunch of time in the morning

Path:

Think about the top thing that you want to get done every single day. It may not be the most important thing that will get done the whole day, but it should be the most important recurring daily task that you have. For me it might be writing a blog post or dealing with customer service for my blogging platform, Sett. Then, every day, track what time you started that activity.

This sounds like it wouldn't have much of an effect, but what it's actually doing is training your subconscious to recognize when you start that task, and to value starting early. Without doing anything else, your schedule will gradually shift up until you're doing high-value tasks first thing in the morning. This habit works on the principle of "what gets measured gets managed."

Notes:

You may find that you rush to get that one task done, but that you then go back to wasting time. This is particularly likely if that first task is something that doesn't take very long or doesn't take a lot of engagement. The solution to this is to start tracking another task alongside it. In practice, I track when I write a blog post and when I start working on Sett. The blog post usually jumps me into productive mode, and then when I start programing for Sett, I usually end up getting into a groove that lasts for hours, or maybe the whole day.

Plan When Stuck

Another leading cause of procrastination is simply not knowing what to do next. This can be the most frustrating form of procrastination, because you're genuinely motivated to work, but you can't actually get yourself to make any progress. The surest sign that this is what's stopping you is when you ask yourself whether or not you know specifically what you should be doing next, and you can't quite put your finger on it.

Pros:
- Eliminates a frustrating mode of procrastination
- Gives you time to zoom out and look at long-term strategy
- Carries over across multiple days

Cons:
- Can lead to another form of procrastination where you plan a lot, but fail to execute

Path:

This habit is triggered by procrastinating, asking yourself if you know exactly what you should be doing next, and failing to come up with a definite answer. Whenever that happens, simply set a clock for thirty minutes, and begin planning.

If you don't do this regularly now, you will feel like it is an enormous waste of time. The first fifteen minutes might be spent writing down absolutely nothing, and feeling like you're compounding the problem by stepping back from the actual work that you should be doing.

But just as a habit won't get built if you don't have proper motivation, useful work won't get done unless you have a clear path for it.

It's often easiest to start with a very long-term vision. Why do you want this goal? What exactly does success look like? A path exists between your current position and almost any goal, but it can only be found if you know what that goal is, and look from a high enough altitude.

Begin to imagine what those paths would look like. Take yourself out of the equation, and think of how someone else might find success. What would his major waypoints be along the way?

Get out a piece of paper and rotate it into landscape mode, so that the long edge is facing you. On the right hand side, write down the end goal. If you're not exactly sure, write down whatever comes to mind. Working back from the right side, write waypoints in chronological order. So things that will have to happen sooner are further towards the left. Finally, use the left hand side as an immediate overloaded todo list. Write down anything you could do next, regardless of whether or not it's the best option available to you.

Keep at this for a full twenty minutes or so. Sometimes you'll be overwhelmed with ideas and your writing hand will have trouble keeping up with your brain. That happens when you're paralyzed by choice and can't decide what to do next. Other times you won't have a single idea at first.

Just fill in the gaps as ideas come. If you're working on immediate todo items and think of a better way to articulate your goal, jump forward and write it down.

You've now drawn a messy and imprecise map of your path towards your goal. Take the final ten minutes of your planning session to read through everything you've written, and try to see the threads that stretch across the page. Which goal do you want most? Which waypoints are you confident on? Which immediate actions could you do an amazing job at?

Only at this stage should you consider crossing things off. You've given your brain the freedom to unload everything it's got, so now you can curate. The goal isn't to figure out the one true path to success, but rather to understand what you're up against. It's this context that allows you to look at your immediate todo items and choose the best, or one of the best, to attack next.

Notes:

This is my way of planning, and I make no claim that it's the absolute best planning method in the world. It works for me and for other people, but you could very easily find something that works better for you. So if you're a list maker, a deep thinker, or someone who needs to bounce ideas off a friend, use your method. The habit is intended to help you get out of the weeds and get perspective on your situation to stimulate progress again.

Rating Your Day

Once I realized that just by tracking the time I started key bits of work every day, I could effortlessly cut out the procrastination that usually preceded them, I began to look for other habits that would work because of the "what gets measured gets managed" principle. One of the most effective was also the most simple: rating each day made my days better.

Pros:
- Improves quality of time spent each day with little effort
- Provides a record of performance

Cons:
- Feels like a waste of time at first
- Doesn't work if not honest about quality of day

Path:

Every night, before you go to bed, rate your day on a scale from one to ten. I recommend that you rate yourself on how little time you wasted, rather than on raw productivity or output. This method has its perils, but the advantage is that you don't have to give yourself a bad rating if you spent the day doing something unproductive but worthwhile, like helping out a friend.

Don't worry about having a consistent scale. Inevitably, your standards will shift as you're increasingly able to use your time efficiently. So you'll give yourself an eight for a day, and when glancing at weeks past you'll remember other days where you earned an eight, and feel like, in retrospect, they were no better than a seven. Historical accuracy isn't all that important, though. The benefit is gained primarily because you'll want to be able to give yourself a good rating at the end of the day, so you'll waste less time trying to earn the rating.

Notes:

I've found rating my day to be very useful when I'm in a slump. When you're in a slump, it can sometimes feel like your previous accomplishments were nothing but flukes, and that you'll never be able to produce good work again. Our memories are emotion-based, which means that when we're frustrated, we can most vividly remember other times during which we were frustrated. When things are going great, all we can think of are other times that things went great.

When you have a few months of rating history, however, you can logically see that slumps never last very long. They feel like they last forever in the moment, but I've never actually had one that lasts more than three or four days. You can also see just how recently you had a great day, and how frequently they come. All of this helps put a slump into context and motivate you to grind your way out, rather than feel helpless.

Putting it All Together

There's a lot to be said about habits, many angles from which to analyze them, and any number of paths towards building them. That can be exciting and motivating, or it can be overwhelming. For all of us, it's probably both of these things at various times.

At its core, though, the practice of building habits is simple. We identify things that we do each day and we adjust them to make them a little bit better. We put our faith in the compounded power of small repeated actions, and we adjust our behavior to reap those benefits.

Compounding requires a long time horizon, which is why I've stressed the importance of beginning with small and manageable habits. A lifelong process of building and maintaining habits is far and away the greatest benefit you can receive from the advice in this book. Starting with humble habits is the best way to make sure you are on that path.

Increasing willpower is a worthy goal, but progress is slow even under the best of conditions. To truly exceed our normal capabilities, we must learn to use that willpower as efficiently as possible. To do that, we habitualize as much as possible, taking actions that previously consumed willpower and making them automatic. This book is called Superhuman by Habit because the results can seem truly superhuman when willpower is leveraged in this manner.

The techniques in this book have been used by me and

many others to increase our health, happiness, productivity, and impact far beyond what could be achieved through willpower and effort alone. Whether they have the same effect for you is entirely your decision. My strongest advice is to choose a habit immediately, commit to it, and begin the journey.

99024751R00068